Intellectual Property

CHANDOS
INTELLECTUAL PROPERTY SERIES

Chandos' new series of books are aimed at intellectual property professionals. They have been specially commissioned to provide the reader with an authoritative view of current thinking. They are designed to provide easy-to-read and (most importantly) practical coverage of topics that are of interest to intellectual property professionals. If you would like a full listing of current and forthcoming titles, please visit our website www.chandospublishing.com or contact Hannah Grace-Williams on email info@chandospublishing.com or telephone number +44 (0) 1865 884447.

New authors: we are always pleased to receive ideas for new titles; if you would like to write a book for Chandos, please contact Dr Glyn Jones on email gjones@chandospublishing.com or telephone number +44 (0) 1865 884447.

Bulk orders: some organisations buy a number of copies of our books. If you are interested in doing this, we would be pleased to discuss a discount. Please contact Hannah Grace-Williams on email info@chandospublishing.com or telephone number +44 (0) 1865 884447.

Intellectual Property

The lifeblood of your company

MARK ELMSLIE
AND
SIMON PORTMAN

Chandos Publishing
Oxford • England

K1401 .E46 2006
0134109533/06

Elmslie, Mark.

Intellectual property :
the lifeblood of your
2006.

2007 02 23

Chandos Publishing (Oxford) Limited
Chandos House
5 & 6 Steadys Lane
Stanton Harcourt
Oxford OX29 5RL
UK
Tel: +44 (0) 1865 884447 Fax: +44 (0) 1865 884448
Email: info@chandospublishing.com
www.chandospublishing.com

First published in Great Britain in 2006

ISBN:
1 84334 135 2 (paperback)
1 84334 181 6 (hardback)

© Mark Elmslie and Simon Portman, 2006

British Library Cataloguing-in-Publication Data.
A catalogue record for this book is available from the British Library.

All rights reserved. No part of this publication may be reproduced, stored in or introduced into a retrieval system, or transmitted, in any form, or by any means (electronic, mechanical, photocopying, recording or otherwise) without the prior written permission of the Publishers. This publication may not be lent, resold, hired out or otherwise disposed of by way of trade in any form of binding or cover other than that in which it is published without the prior consent of the Publishers. Any person who does any unauthorised act in relation to this publication may be liable to criminal prosecution and civil claims for damages.

The Publishers make no representation, express or implied, with regard to the accuracy of the information contained in this publication and cannot accept any legal responsibility or liability for any errors or omissions.

The material contained in this publication constitutes general guidelines only and does not represent to be advice on any particular matter. No reader or purchaser should act on the basis of material contained in this publication without first taking professional advice appropriate to their particular circumstances.

The right of Simon Portman and Mark Elmslie to be identified as the authors of this work have been asserted by them in accordance with the Copyright, Designs and Patents Act, 1988.

Printed in the UK and USA.

Printed in the UK by 4edge Limited - www.4edge.co.uk

Contents

Foreword ix
Acknowledgements xi
About the authors xiii

1 Introduction 1
   What this book is about 1
   What is intellectual property? 2
   Terminology 3
   Why is intellectual property important? 3

2 Different types of intellectual property and related rights 7
   Patents 9
   Designs 16
   Registered trade marks 21
   Copyright 28
   Passing off 36
   Domain names 41
   Confidential information and know-how 44
   Supplementary protection certificates 47
   Data exclusivity 48
   Semiconductor topography rights 50
   Remedies 51

3 Dealing in IP rights 55
   Overview 55
   Assignments 56
   Licences 57
   Confidentiality agreements 58
   Materials transfer agreements 60

	Heads of agreement	61
	Options	63
	Manufacturing agreements	64
	Research agreements	66
	Collaboration agreements	71
	Commercial licences	74
	Liability and legality	79
	Disputes, law and jurisdiction	80
	Negotiating contracts	82
4	**Good intellectual property maintenance and management**	**85**
	Protection of owned and generated rights	85
	Patent and trade mark attorneys	87
	Ownership of internally generated intellectual property	88
	Ownership of externally generated intellectual property	89
	Keeping information confidential	92
	Protecting against infringement of others' rights	93
	General awareness and training	95
	Meta-tags and websites generally	96
	Summary	97
5	**Dealing with intellectual property disputes**	**99**
	Introduction	99
	Nature of litigation	99
	The English system and interrelationship with other parts of Europe	100
	The Civil Procedure Rules	101
	Pre-action correspondence	105
	The courts	108
	Offers to settle	109
	Alternative dispute resolution	111
	Insurance	113
	Some checkpoints prior to litigation being initiated	114
	Interim orders	115

	Security for costs	116
	Documents: privilege and disclosure	117
	A final word	118
6	**Issues arising on change of ownership**	**119**
	Sale of business or change of control?	119
	Questions that will be asked	120
	IP contract issues	121
	Due diligence and warranties	123
	How to make the process easier	124
7	**How does IP affect your business in practice?**	**127**
	Introduction	127
	Bioscience	128
	Software	132
	Consumer goods	136
8	**Conclusion**	**139**
Appendix: Useful websites		**141**
Index		**147**

Foreword

By Peter Hewkin of Cambridge Network

Ideas change the world, and Cambridge, where the authors of this book are based, is a prime example of this. Over the centuries the discovery of gravity, the invention of the jet engine and unravelling the structure of DNA are all traceable to Cambridge scientists.

More recently the Cambridge phenomenon is all about making money out of ideas. In the last 40 years Europe's most significant cluster of knowledge-based companies has sprung up in Cambridge and the surrounding region. Many started with little more than an idea. Some have grown to the point where they have floated in the UK or USA – reaching $1 billion capitalisations.

As a consequence intellectual property has not only always been at the heart of Cambridge, it is something which is of particular relevance to its business community. It is only natural then that one of the City's own law firms, which itself played a part in the Cambridge phenomenon, should have developed a leading reputation in the IP field over the years.

This book, by Mark Elmslie and Simon Portman, may have been conceived in Cambridge but its relevance is universal. It carries the key messages of the need to recognise, protect and successfully exploit a company's IP, in relation to both the technology which makes its products and processes work and the branding which helps market them.

Intellectual Property

I would like to claim that the Cambridge phenomenon is unique. I can't. Rather it represents one of the best examples of innovation, invention and entrepreneurship which have always been the hallmark of the commercial vitality of this country as a whole. The success of the Cambridge phenomenon is mirrored by that of other technology clusters across the UK.

In writing this book Simon and Mark have distilled the essence of the value of IP for business – a value which is central for commercial enterprise everywhere.

Peter Hewkin

Acknowledgements

Thanks to Niel Ackermann, Mary Kasanicki and Daniel Hon for their research and contributions, and to Sandra Blatch for doing most of the typing.

About the authors

Mark Elmslie gained an LLB at the University of Adelaide, and an LLM at the University of London. He has specialised in non-contentious and contentious intellectual property law since 1990 and leads the highly regarded IP litigation practice at Hewitsons in Cambridge.

Mark worked with London firms for 12 years, including more than three years as a partner and latterly as head of the IP group of a well-known London firm, before returning in 2000 to his native Australia to become special counsel in the IP group of the nationwide practice Minter Ellison. He joined Hewitsons as a partner in 2002.

Mark has extensive experience in intellectual property law and has conducted major litigation both here and in Australia for UK and international clients across the whole spectrum of IP work. He has a particular interest and experience in brand protection work and Internet-related litigation. He also has extensive experience in licensing, brand portfolio management, collaborative research agreements and other agreements concerned with vesting and exploitation of intellectual property rights. Mark regularly writes and speaks on intellectual property law.

The author may be contacted at:
   Tel: 01223 532720
   E-mail: *markelmslie@hewitsons.com*

Simon Portman first gained a degree in Classics at Merton College, Oxford but subsequently took legal qualifications at London Guildhall University and trained at the London law firm of Boodle Hatfield. His time there included a secondment to Shell International which gave him valuable experience of industry.

He has worked at the leading Cambridge law firm Hewitsons since 1997 and is a partner in the firm heading up the highly rated bioscience team. He advises companies, individuals and institutions on a wide range of legal, contractual and intellectual property issues. He also sits on the Intellectual Property Advisory Committee of the Bioindustry Association.

Simon is the author of numerous articles for industry and legal publications including *Managing Intellectual Property* and *Patent World*, and is co-author of *Commercial Issues for Lifescience Companies* (Monitor Press, 2000). He also regularly gives seminars and workshops on legal and commercial issues in the UK and across Europe.

The author may be contacted at:

Tel: 01223 532705
E-mail: *simonportman@hewitsons.com*

1

Introduction

What this book is about

Intellectual property is everywhere. It flows through every aspect of the life of a business, and it can make it or break it. Over the years we have been practising law, IP has moved from being a backwater area of practice to a major field. From biotech start-ups to the most famous branded companies, it is difficult to think of an industry in which IP in one of its many forms is not truly the lifeblood of the company.

This is a practical book for businesses, not a technical book for lawyers. While we have identified what we mean by IP, we have not analysed it in depth or dealt in detail with the plethora of different regimes that apply. We also primarily deal with the UK system. Other countries have different systems, although the broad principles remain the same. This book is intended to assist those in business to arrive at a better understanding of how intellectual property impacts on their business and how they can better use it to make money.

We begin with an analysis of the principles and nature of IP, how it applies to different types of business, and why it is often the most valuable of a company's assets and the hardest to protect. We move on to describe the different types of intellectual property rights, beginning with patents, designs and trade marks, and moving through the different specialist fields of IP.

Next comes the exploitation of IP rights, and the various issues arising on selling, licensing and other dealings in IP. We then look at the maintenance of IP, keeping rights properly registered, enforcing them and dealing with disputes, and the issues arising on the disposal or acquisition by a business of its IP rights. Finally, we move on to look at examples of the practical application and use of IP in three different types of business and how IP impacts on them.

What is intellectual property?

The term 'intellectual property' covers a range of personal property rights attaching to various products of the human mind. It is intangible (i.e. does not attach to any physical object) and as a result intellectual property rights are not enforceable by possession but by action. In other words, a party holding those rights can, if it has the inclination (and the money), take action to prevent someone else who has no rights over that intellectual property from using it.

Different IP rights attach to different types of property (see Chapter 2). Some of these rights are registered (i.e. the owner must apply for and be granted the right in question) and some are unregistered (i.e. they arise naturally and need not be applied for). Some are generally applicable; others are only relevant to narrow technical sectors. The global term 'intellectual property' is used to cover all of these rights, even though they may differ from one another significantly. You may also have encountered the term 'industrial property' which used to be viewed as covering patents, trade marks and designs but not copyright. However, the two terms intellectual property and industrial property now tend to be viewed as meaning the same thing.

Intellectual property law works within the legal landscape and the existence and exercise of intellectual property rights may be affected by other areas of law. For example, competition law often has a substantial effect on aspects of intellectual property, since intellectual property revolves around the creation of exclusive rights and this can lead to anti-competitive behaviour. Striking a balance between these two regimes has always been difficult. This area of law is a separate subject in itself and beyond the scope of this book, but the reader should be aware that it (and other areas of law) have this potential application to IP.

Terminology

In this book we use the terms 'IP' and 'intellectual property' to refer to the more formal rights such as patents and trade marks, as well as rights some would regard as not falling strictly within this area, such as the right to protect confidential information. References to 'patent attorney' and 'trade mark attorney' are to professionals who are not solicitors but who advise on registration issues in connection with patents, registered designs and trade marks.

Why is intellectual property important?

The concept of intellectual property rights arises from the need to reward innovation and creativity. Society obviously needs innovators and creators to improve our quality of life through the development of new technology, improved and new products and the arts. However, very few creators and innovators are entirely altruistic. They often require a financial incentive to come up with new ideas. This will only be possible if they are guaranteed some sort of monetary reward for what they have done. The best way of ensuring this is to provide that for a set period no one can exploit those rights without the creator's permission, which enables the creator to demand payment in return for that permission. For example, few people would be inclined to put the time and effort into writing a book if, immediately it was finished, anyone could reproduce and supply it, since then the author would get no financial reward.

Intellectual property rights have become more important as time has gone by, particularly in view of the technological revolution of the last century. It used to be the case that a company's value primarily resided in its physical assets. However, technological advances and the advent of technology itself as an industry mean that in many sectors the bulk of a company's money is spent on developing its products or processes; once a product has been developed it can often be manufactured easily and quickly using an automated process and cheap raw materials. For example, millions of dollars and many years might be invested in developing a successful cancer drug, but once developed it may merely comprise a small pill that can be churned out fairly easily. Without IP protection, the company which developed it would then see others 'piggybacking' off its inventiveness, making money by easily producing and selling something which they have spent no money developing. In such circumstances, most of the company's value will reside in what it has created and its potential to create more products and/or processes in the sector.

As well as becoming more important in recent years, both the concept of intellectual property as a whole and the different types of intellectual property protection available have been challenged by and had to adapt to new technologies. For example, computer software and biotechnology were not even conceived of when the first intellectual property rights were born. Such new technology has either had to be shoehorned into existing intellectual property rights or to have a new category of intellectual property right created especially for it. Either option has had its pros and cons. Furthermore, the arrival of the Internet and the digital age, making unauthorised dissemination and copying so easy that in many cases they cannot be effectively policed, has led some to question whether there is still a place for intellectual property rights at all.

Finally, intellectual property has given rise to serious ethical concerns. Relying on patent protection could, it has been alleged, enable a company to create a monopoly and squeeze out the competition, which stifles future innovation by others and is bad news for end users and the industry in question generally. It has also been claimed that patenting drugs enables pharmaceutical companies to charge whatever price they like, which may make those drugs too expensive in the Third World where they are needed most. However, returning to our earlier point, the absence of intellectual property would stifle the urge to innovate which would ultimately prejudice everybody, rich or poor, big or small.

2

Different types of intellectual property and related rights

This is in itself a vast subject, and we will not be attempting to examine all the IP rights in depth but rather to give the reader guidance as to major features of the different rights. There are various ways of analysing the operation of the different rights. One is to draw a distinction between registered rights (such as registered trade marks, patents and registered designs) and unregistered rights (such as the right to prevent passing off, unregistered design right and copyright).

In examining these rights it is helpful to look at what these different rights *do* – what do the rights aim to protect? Patents and for the most part designs aim to protect industrially applied items. Copyright protects created (but not necessarily creative) skill and labour as manifested in material across the whole field of human activity but with limited applicability (for purely practical reasons) in industrially applied goods, and passing off and trade mark law, along with other parts of what we might loosely call 'trading law', protect what the law will regard as unfair trading, with the aim of stopping the consumer from being misled and the businessman from having his hard-won reputation interfered with or profited from.

It is also helpful to look at some 'rights' that are not in

the traditional sense intellectual property rights at all but which can nevertheless be extremely valuable assets of a company, such as domain names and know-how.

This chapter details various categories of intellectual property rights, the criteria which must be met for them to apply, how one acquires them and what sort of protection they afford. We firstly deal with registered intellectual property rights (which must be applied for), then unregistered rights (which arise naturally). Next we look at the more recent types of intellectual property rights which only apply to certain kinds of technology. Finally, we shall look at the common remedies available following the infringement of these rights.

Thus the order of this chapter is:

- registered rights:
    - patents
    - designs
    - trade marks
- unregistered rights and claims:
    - copyright
    - passing off
    - domain names
    - confidential information and know-how
- IP rights applying to some specific technologies:
    - supplementary protection certificates
    - data exclusivity
    - semiconductor topography rights
- remedies for infringing intellectual property rights.

Patents

Background and definition

A patent is an intellectual property right over an invention which gives the holder a monopoly right to prevent others from making use of the invention described by its claims. Patents last for 20 years and give the owner exclusivity during this period. In return, the inventor discloses his invention to the public which is free to use it after the end of the life of the patent.

Like other registered intellectual property rights, patents are granted on application to patent registries operated by different countries. In the United Kingdom, applications are made for patents through the Patent Office in Newport, South Wales. In addition, an applicant can apply for a European patent with the European Patent Office, which grants a bundle of national patents for designated member states of the European Patent Convention. Finally, an 'international' application can be made under the Patent Cooperation Treaty; the application will then proceed in the patent offices of different member countries. Under an international agreement, in nearly all cases an application will give an applicant 'priority' for other applications. This means the filing date is in effect backdated to the first 'priority' application.

A proposal for a single European Community patent has been made but not yet put in place. This section deals with United Kingdom patents, but the reader should be aware the rules for others can be different. Your patent attorney will usually have a working knowledge of the systems of some other major industrial countries, but local advice will be needed for any substantive issues.

Structure

A patent application is a document containing a specification, which is a description of the background to and nature of the claimed invention, followed by a series of 'claims' – what the invention claims as its ambit. The claims define and limit the invention. Their purpose is to concisely describe the invention in order to form a boundary or what is sometimes called a 'ring fence' around the invention so that anyone reading the specification and claims can understand the limit of the invention and avoid crossing that boundary.

What is patentable?

Patents will be granted for useful, new inventions. There are a number of exclusions. Discoveries, business methods, methods of presenting information, dramatic, literary, musical and artistic works and computer programs are among the classes of material excluded from patent protection. Inventions can be manifested in processes or products. A patent might be granted over anything from an invention for a new and useful piece of agricultural machinery to methods of manufacture of hormones to systems created by clever software (as opposed to the program itself).

The boundaries of what is patentable are always being tested and examined. Science and business are constantly seeking to extend what can be patented and issues such as public morality and the need to prevent patenting of naturally occurring phenomena play a significant part in determining what is and is not patentable.

Software

In the USA, there is increasing scope to patent software and even business methods despite the fact that many of these methods on the face of it seem fairly generic. There is less scope for this in Europe on the basis that such creations do not have a requisite industrial application. Nevertheless, if a computer program is used as part of the implementation of an invention, a patent can be acquired for the invention as a whole.

Gene patents

Patents for gene sequences are subject to the same criteria of novelty, non-obviousness and industrial application as any other patent. However, concerns have been raised that ownership of a patent in a genetic sequence is in some way ownership of part of the human body. This view is incorrect, since the Biotechnology Directive (which was intended by the European Commission to be implemented across member states to harmonise patent practice throughout Europe) does not deviate from the criteria for patentability outlined above.

The Directive sets out, as a prerequisite for patentability, that a gene must have been isolated from the human body by means of a technical process or have been developed *in vitro*. Individual countries' governments have, in some member states, implemented the Directive into national law in accordance with national policy rather than wholesale, which means that it has not been adopted consistently; for example, Italy has refused to implement the Biotechnology Directive into its law and Germany has implemented the Directive with some variations.

Applying the criteria for patentability, the rapid advances in biotechnology have meant that techniques which were once cutting-edge have now become commonplace and potentially obvious. This is particularly true in the case of research into genetic material, where isolation of DNA sequences has become more straightforward. This change has been reflected in the scope of the patents which have been granted for gene sequences. Historically, these have been very broad and a patent for a gene sequence has included all variants. However, more recently, where a fragment of an amino acid sequence is known, the sequence of the DNA has been considered to be obvious and therefore unpatentable.

Stem cell patents

Stem cells are cells which have the potential to develop into a variety of cell types. They are considered to be clinically important as potential treatments for diseases and injuries where there is a need to renew or replace tissue. However, the patenting of stem cells is currently a highly controversial area of patent law. Some campaigners suggest that stem cells should be unpatentable on the grounds of immorality when the stem cells are derived from human embryos. As was said above, there is also a lack of consistency in Europe regarding the interpretation of the Biotechnology Directive, which sets out the framework for the patentability of stem cells. In the UK, the Patent Office has taken the view that established adult stem cell lines are patentable, and more controversially, that pluripotent stem cell lines (stem cells which have the potential to develop into many, but not all, cell types) from human embryos are also patentable. It is not possible to patent totipotent stem cells (stem cells which have the capability of developing into a human being).

However, the European Patent Office has come to the opposite view. Interpreting the Biotechnology Directive more broadly, the EPO has ruled that stem cells isolated from embryos are not patentable on the grounds that the invention was developed by the use of human embryos for industrial or commercial purposes.

The variability in interpretation of the Biotechnology Directive means that the legal environment in the UK, where the Directive has been adopted in its entirety, is much more friendly towards innovation by companies wishing to carry out stem cell research than in many other countries in Europe.

Fundamental rules of patentability

In order to be patentable, the subject matter of the application must be new, non-obvious and useful in industry. Questions of novelty and obviousness are legal and technical questions.

Many patent applications fail or patents granted are subsequently revoked on the basis that the invention is not 'new' because the applicant has publicly disclosed the invention before the application is made. If the invention is already known, it is not new. Any discussions or negotiations relating to a potential patent or the subject matter of a patent should be kept confidential by means of properly constructed confidentiality agreements or arrangements prepared by a suitably qualified lawyer.

The second primary rule is that the invention must not be 'obvious'. It must have some inventive aspect to it. It must be something which is not only new but possessed of an inventive element, a quality which will be recognised by someone experienced in the field as being a real step forward in the area.

One key determinant is whether the invention is a

commercial success. That often (but not always) tells whether it is new and inventive.

The process of application

Your patent attorney will advise concerning the often complex decision-making processes as to where to apply, what invention(s) to apply for, and the costs and nature of the process involved. Like trade mark applications, patent applications are filed (with the Patent Office) and after a period of examination 'published', which means made available for public examination. Following publication, competitors and other interested parties may attack the application and seek to have it refused. The period between filing and publication of the application is normally about 18 months. Once granted, a patent can be revoked on various grounds. Patent applications can be very expensive, with the cost rising sharply if applications in different countries are pursued (the applications will sometimes need to be translated into more than one language and this in itself is very expensive). It is difficult to give an average cost for an application, but a simple straightforward application in the UK might cost £2,000 including patent attorney fees. Most cost substantially more.

Term

As mentioned above, a patent lasts for 20 years from the date of filing and renewal fees are payable periodically. If a patent has been granted by the European Patent Office or proceeds via an international application it separates into a bundle of national patents, each of which must be maintained. The rules concerning term vary with different countries.

Dealings with patents

As with other registered intellectual property rights, patents are pieces of property. They can be mortgaged, licensed or sold. They can be owned jointly or individually. The first owner of a patent is the inventor, but arrangements can be made for the ownership to be vested in a company or some other entity. All transactions should be registered with the Patent Office.

If an invention is generated in the course of employment by an employee, the employer will become the owner of the patent, but an employee has the right to seek compensation if the patent or a product made according to it is commercially successful (although to our knowledge no one has ever succeeded in such an application).

Companies often license patents and there are companies which own vast stables of patents and make their money by licensing them out. Licences are dealt with elsewhere in this book and can take a variety of forms. Licences can confer a right to sue infringers.

Infringements

Infringement actions are notoriously expensive. Many patent disputes are resolved peacefully by commercial common sense because both parties realise that it is in no one's interest to fight a case out in court. A patent is infringed once a patented article or process is imported, made, used, sold, etc. without licence or permission. There are various exceptions and qualifications to this rule, for example relating to private or experimental use. The court will need to decide if the article falls within the claims of the patent. Whether a patent has been infringed in any particular instance will often be a very technical question. Speaking generally, even if the competitor's product does not fit literally within the claims, if a person skilled in the particular area of technology would have understood the language of the claims to include the offending article then the patent will be infringed. Once infringement is established, damages can be claimed from publication date.

Patent infringement actions usually involve a claim by the patent holder of infringement and a counter-claim by the alleged infringer that the patent is invalid and should never have been granted. As well as being expensive, patent actions are notoriously time-consuming and smaller competitors are usually at a disadvantage to larger companies with substantial funds to fight claims. Although attempts have been made to address this, the problem remains and because of its expense patent litigation in the United Kingdom is usually engaged in only by large companies. See Chapter 5 on dispute resolution.

Designs

Introduction

Designs law relates to two separate areas, registered and unregistered designs

Designs have substantial similarities to patents in that they are primarily directed to protection for industrial articles or concepts. However, designs can apply to protect goods created to be attractive to the eye. Some aspects of designs law are similar to copyright, protecting against copying, and some have more in common with patents law, protecting the area covered or 'ring-fenced' by the design.

Different types of IP and related rights

It is an expanding and ever more used area of law and is expected to become much more utilised by industry in the future, having substantial cost advantages over patents. Designs law can protect such diverse articles as the shape of the sole of a shoe, an attractive mass-produced lamp, aspects of a car body, toys and pig pens.

Registered designs

The system which now operates in the UK provides protection for a *design* as opposed to the article in which it is incorporated. So protection is conferred for the design across any product to which it is applied. The system has radically changed in recent years. As a result of an EU directive on the subject, the UK registered designs law has been substantially rewritten and now applies the same set of criteria as the new Community registered design, the latter applying across the whole of the EU. Applications for UK registered designs are made in the UK at the Patent Office and applications for EU registered designs at the Office for the Harmonisation of the Internal Market (OHIM), in Alicante Spain (see *http://oami.eu.int/en/design/default.htm*).

'Design' is defined as:

> the appearance of the whole or a part of a product resulting from the features of, in particular, the lines, contours, colours, shape, texture or materials of the product or its ornamentation.

A 'Product' is defined as:

> any industrial or handicraft item other than a computer program; and, in particular, includes packaging, get-up, graphic symbols, typographic typefaces and parts intended to be assembled into a complex product.

In order for a design to be registrable it must be 'new' and have 'individual character'. 'New' is a similar concept to that which exists in patent law (above), although there are differences. It is the 'design' that must be novel, so if it appears incorporated in some other product it is not novel.

There are exceptions to novelty in relation to disclosures

- in confidence;
- which could not reasonably have become known in the normal course of business to people carrying on business in the European Economic Area in the field concerned;
- made by the designer, his successor in title, someone who learns of it from either, or by someone acting against the rights of the designer or his successor in title (i.e. without agreement), within the 12 months before the date of the application.

It is necessary in looking at individual character to ask if the design produces a different 'overall impression' on what would be an 'informed user' from that of any previous design. This is a new test and is rather oddly worded. It remains to be seen how it is to be applied but it would appear to be quite a high hurdle.

Design registration does not exist in features of appearance which are solely dictated by a product's technical function. In addition no rights will exist in features of the appearance of the design which are necessary for it to be connected to, placed in, against or around another product so either can perform its function. Thus the visual aspect of the design is the important one.

There is an exception to protection, namely design features relating to assembly of a modular system. This will apply to toy products designed to fit together in the same way as a Lego system does.

Different types of IP and related rights

The first owner of a registered design will be the person who commissioned the design and if made in the course of employment the employer will own it. The right has to be renewed every five years, will normally last a maximum of 25 years and can be granted to any applicant whether located in the EU or not. As with patents, registered designs can be licensed or assigned and there is a statutory framework. As with patents it is important to register transactions.

A registered design is infringed by the use of a design which does not produce on the informed user a different overall impression, taking into account the degree of freedom of the designer in developing his design. Note the negative, and rather odd, phrasing of the test. It is important to remember that the use does not have to be of the same article – it is the design which is protected.

Unregistered design rights

The EU and UK systems part company when it comes to dealing with unregistered rights. In the UK we have from 1989 had a separate and unique 'unregistered design right' (UDR) which incorporates elements of copyright and design law to give a special form of protection for industrially applied articles.

Community unregistered design right (CUDR)

This system is intended to work in cooperation with the Community registered design system. Broadly this right applies to the same designs as does the registered system but only for three years. It is intended to provide a link with the registered rights system which is voluntary. It is recognised that many designs are of short duration and not worth the cost of registration; this gives the designer the option of registering the rights. The key difference is that in order to infringe a CUDR it must be copied. That is not a requirement for Community registered design right.

UK unregistered design

Finally, some designs are given a copyright type protection by the UK unregistered design right. As mentioned above this applies only in the UK and it applies to any aspect of the shape or configuration of an article. It does not apply to surface decoration. In order to qualify a design must be original, which means 'not copied', but also it must not be 'commonplace in the design field in question'. Methods or principles of construction are excluded and designs which enable an article to match with another or enable an article to fit with another are excluded. Ownership vests in the commissioner if made for money or money's worth and in the employer if made in the course of employment. Only EU citizens and certain specified others (not including those from the US) can qualify for ownership. The period of protection is 15 years from the date the design is made or recorded or ten years after making products to the design.

Infringement occurs when there is copying. As in copyright (see below), there are two types of infringement. Primary infringement occurs when there is copying of the design. Secondary infringement broadly means dealing in infringing copies. The defendant will have a defence if he can show he did not know or have reason to believe he was dealing in an infringing copy. As with registered designs, there is an innocence defence in relation to damages. The usual remedies apply (see below).

Licences of right and designs

British unregistered design right is subject to a 'licence of right' provision, which means in effect a licence has to be given on terms during the last five years of the right. The terms can be settled by order or agreement. Registered designs and Community UDR do not have licence of right provisions.

Registered trade marks

Background

The current trade mark registration system applying in the UK was implemented by the Trade Marks Act 1994, enacted following a European Community Directive. The system works broadly along the lines of the European Community Trade Mark ('CTM') system. The old law applying in the UK had been existence for many years and the new one broadened considerably what can be registered. Trade marks and brands generally are playing an increasingly important role in the process of making and selling products.

Different systems

In deciding whether to register a company name or product name as a trade mark the primary issue is often cost. Broadly there are three paths. One can apply solely in the UK under the UK Trade Marks Act, in the European Community countries for a CTM, or via an international agreement called the Madrid Protocol for registration in (and from) a multiplicity of countries throughout the world. Some combination of these courses may be appropriate.

If it is intended that the mark will only ever be used in the UK then obviously filing for protection beyond the UK would not be appropriate. However, especially with new businesses or products the extent of the potential market is often unknown and it may be necessary to review any decision further along the road, bearing in mind that by that time the mark may not be registrable in any target county. A system of priority allows an applicant in most other target countries to backdate the application by up to six months to the date of the earlier application.

UK and CTM applications are made direct to the Registration Office in the UK (at the Patent Office in Newport, South Wales), or at the Community Trade Mark Office (in Alicante, Spain) (see *http://oami.eu.int/en/mark/default.htm*). An application via the Madrid Protocol is made in any local country registry and then proceeds in the selected registry of other chosen countries via a central office in Geneva.

Which route or combination of routes is taken will often depend on cost and it is important to ascertain the cost before proceeding. It is also important to periodically review any decision. We look below at the UK system, which operates in a similar way to the CTM.

Different types of trade marks

As mentioned above, the 1994 Act substantially broadened the definition of registered trade marks. The definition is:

> any sign capable of being represented graphically which is capable of distinguishing goods or services of one undertaking from those of other undertakings.

More specifically trade marks may include:

words (including personal names), designs, letters, numerals or the shape of goods or their packaging.

Note that the reference is to goods or services (service marks). References in this book to 'trade marks' include both.

One can apply to register colours and even smells and sounds on the basis that they function as 'trade marks'. These are the exception. Most businesses will be concerned with more practical questions, such as whether their business name can be registered and how much it will cost. While it is important to remember that the definition of what can be registrable is broad, it is also important to keep in mind the fundamental task which any trade mark must achieve, and that is to distinguish the goods or services of your business from those of your existing and future competitors.

There is a tension, a counterplay, between names which are descriptive of the product or some benefit of the product and names which bear no relationship to it. The latter make for better trade marks because they do not *describe* the goods and thus have a greater *capacity to distinguish*. Although it will take work in advertising, marketing and other forms of brand promotion to develop the trade mark, it has a far greater capacity to perform its function than one with any descriptive qualities. 'Kodak' (a made up word) is a superb trade mark, having no connection whatsoever to the products it denotes and thus has an instantly recognisable and memorable capacity to distinguish. However, a trade mark which alludes to the product or some quality of it (e.g. 'Comfort' for fabric conditioner, 'Rentokil' for pest extermination) is often the preferred choice.

Trade marks which are purely descriptive are generally not registrable and the more descriptive the trade mark, the harder it is to show that it is capable of distinguishing. So a trade mark which has descriptive elements might nevertheless be registrable with evidence that the public recognise it as signifying the goods come from that producer.

Consult with your trade mark attorney. Do so before selecting a trade mark as he will guide you towards something which is good for the market and is likely to be registrable.

The application

An application has to specify which goods and services (and there may be more than one) the application relates to. It is necessary for an applicant to state that he intends to use the mark in relation to these goods and services but not to demonstrate that he has done so, and an application which is made in bad faith will be refused or a mark registered in contravention of the bad faith provisions will be removed. Once an application is made it passes through an examination process after which it is published in the *Trade Marks Journal* and there is a three-month period during which an interested party can oppose the application. If it passes these hurdles the mark is registered. Typically in the UK a straightforward application will proceed to registration within three to six months, and a straightforward Community trade mark application will normally reach registration within 12 to 18 months. These periods vary substantially, depending on any oppositions or other obstacles to registration. The Register for UK and CTMs is divided into 45 classes of which 34 are for different types of goods and 11 for different types of services, under an internationally agreed classification system.

Once registered a mark lasts for ten years and is renewable indefinitely provided the renewal fees are paid.

Costs of application

As mentioned above, you should consult with your trade mark attorney about costs. Like any legal process it is not possible to state with certainty what the costs will be because it may depend on unforeseen events such as opposition by competitors as the application travels through the process. The costs of a straightforward UK trade mark application will vary but on average are around £600 to £800 while the costs of a straightforward Community trade mark application will be around £1,100. Generally the more classes applied for, the higher the cost, and a mark may of course be refused or successfully opposed.

The costs of other applications will vary depending on the country and you should consult with your local trade mark attorney, who will be familiar with these costs. Although it is possible to use the Registry yourself, and indeed the Registry will offer assistance to applicants in person, we always recommend the use of a suitably qualified trade mark attorney.

Using trade marks

A trade mark, like a patent, is an item of property and the Act regulates dealings in trade marks such as assignments, mortgages and licences. Trade marks can be owned by one or more companies or people and are commonly licensed. There are rules governing the validity of assignments and licences. These must follow a prescribed formula. Trade mark licensing is dealt with in more detail elsewhere. As a general point it is worth mentioning that trade marks are often the most valuable part of any business and are some of the most valuable assets in the world (e.g. Coca-Cola, Microsoft, Nike). Management of trade marks is essential to the way they are owned, used and licensed in order to protect them as business assets.

The owners of powerful brands have systems and procedures in place to ensure that their trade marks do not become used to describe the products of others by careful and appropriate application of a variety of enforcement measures. These include the use of Customs officers, trading standards officers and, where appropriate, solicitors' cease and desist letters, and as a last resort litigation (see Chapter 5)

In addition, a trade mark proprietor should take steps to ensure that the trade mark is not used in such a way as to become generic, that is where it becomes used to describe all products of the same type, for example the mark 'Linoleum'. One way trade mark owners do this is by periodically vetting dictionaries to ensure that the word mark does not pass into common descriptive usage.

Refusal of registration

There are various technical grounds on which a trade mark application can be refused. The most important of these is that it is not distinctive of the goods in relation to which the application is made. In addition, trade marks which operate to describe the kind, quality or other descriptive aspect of the goods or services will not be registered. Also, a mark which is too similar to an earlier trade mark whether registered or unregistered or which conflicts with some earlier intellectual property right will not be registered. There are special rules about the registration of shapes of goods or their packaging.

Revocation

If a mark is registrable at the time the application was made

Different types of IP and related rights

but subsequently ceased to operate in the way a trade mark needs to in order to function as a trade mark it may be liable to be removed from the Register and thus become ineffective. If a trade mark has not been used for a period of five years it can also be removed from the Register. If a mark has become descriptive or generic (see above) it can be removed.

Infringement

A trade mark will be infringed in the following circumstances. The terminology speaks of the use of a *sign* infringing a *trade mark*.

- First, if the sign is identical to the mark and used in relation to goods or services which are also identical there is infringement.

- Second, there will be infringement where there is only similarity between the goods or services and/or similarity between sign and mark. In this case the claimant needs to show that there is a 'likelihood of confusion on the part of the public' by which is meant confusion as to the origin of the goods or services.

- Next, a trade mark with a 'reputation' in the UK will be infringed by the use of the same or a similar sign where the use without due course takes unfair advantage of or is detrimental to the distinctive character or repute of the mark. This test contains a number of hurdles ('reputation', 'unfair advantage', etc.) the precise extent of which are determined by case law.

- Finally, there is a comparative advertising provision. Broadly speaking comparative advertising using someone else's trade mark is permissible, provided that the use is

27

honest and does not seek to take unfair advantage or damage the distinctive character or repute of the mark.

This then in a nutshell is a list of the types of infringement which can occur. In addition there is protection for international marks. The proprietor of a qualifying 'well known' trade mark may prevent the use in the UK of an identical or similar mark in relation to identical or similar goods or services where the use is likely to cause confusion. 'Well known' is a high standard.

Like passing off (see below) trade mark infringement does not have any element of intention. Whether the use of a sign infringes a registered trade mark is often a technical question. We deal below with common remedies available for infringement of intellectual property rights and other common themes.

Making good use of your trade mark attorney

Finally, and perhaps most importantly, as we have emphasised elsewhere, ensure that you make good use of your trade mark attorney. These experts work every day within the world of registered trade marks, an area you as a commercial person will only deal in once or twice in your career. As with lawyers it is important to make *intelligent* use of this resource and always keep an eye on what costs are being incurred.

Copyright

This is one of the most long-standing forms of intellectual property right. Copyright is the right of a creator of a qualifying 'copyright work' to prevent others from copying it or a substantial part of it. It applies across a vast range of different types of material and arises automatically. There is no need for registration. In general it applies to protect creative works (for example books, plays and films) as opposed to works of industrial application, such as designs for machined parts. Hence the term of protection (life of the author plus 70 years) is much longer than for the rights that usually apply to protect industrial designs. That said, copyright does apply to protect many commercial items, for example computer code. Although this is not something one would naturally describe as a literary work, it qualifies on this basis.

So copyright applies across a vast range of different types of work and gives a long form of protection.

In order to qualify for protection, a work must be 'original'. In this context this means 'not copied'. So I and my neighbour could independently create a copyright work the same or substantially the same, and so long as there was no (direct or indirect) copying each work would be 'original'. This can be contrasted to 'new' in patent law (see above); there the comparison is with all material anywhere in the world whether known or not. To attract protection, a work does not have to be especially 'creative'. Only a low level of originality is needed. Thus a simple drawing lacking any real artistic merit would normally attract copyright protection. The law does not judge what can and cannot be protected in this way, otherwise what would qualify would depend on taste. However, some substance is needed – slogans or short poems can qualify for protection, but single made-up words would normally not do so.

Because copyright is not registered in the UK and arises on creation or publication of the work, there are sometimes problems with proving when it was created and by whom. The time of creation and the precise extent of the claim can be vital. Hence posting a copy of the copyright work to oneself (and leaving it unopened) or sending a copy to some third party such as a solicitor is often used to provide evidence should it be needed later as to what was created and when. In some other countries such as the US copyright is usually registered.

What does copyright apply to protect?

As mentioned above copyright applies to protect *works*. Copyright is defined and limited by a statute called the Copyright, Designs and Patents Act 1988. Copyright protection is available to:

- literary, dramatic, musical and artistic works;
- sound recordings, films and broadcasts (which include cablecasts);
- the typographic arrangement of published editions.

In addition copyright and a special type of right called database right (see below) apply to protect certain databases.

Thus a novel might be protectable as a literary work, and if turned into a play will become protectable as a dramatic work (the play as performed), a musical work (the music accompanying it) and a sound recording (a recorded version of the play performed on radio). It will be seen that a number of different overlapping copyrights can subsist in the same work, or an adaption of it.

Although all of the different types of rights can be important, literary and artistic works are often most significant to business. Sometimes items produced and sold by a business qualify as an 'artistic work' and thus gain greater protection than industrial designs might afford. Architect's plans can qualify for protection. A set of instructions for the operation of machinery, or images of a company's products (whether produced by any means, such as photography or line drawing), and whether appearing in printed material or other media, for example on the Internet, might qualify for copyright protection. Copyright claims are often brought in conjunction with other claims for infringement of intellectual property rights in relation to specific aspects of the product or material accompanying it.

Qualification and term

Generally, as mentioned above, copyright last 70 years plus the life of the author. It is an extremely long period, especially when compared to patents and other registered rights. Some feel it is too long.

Copyright protection depends on the nationality of the author or the country in which it is first published. There are international agreements to harmonise subsistence and protection, and we recognise copyright arising in and owned by companies in other countries, including in particular the United States. Whether any particular work qualifies for copyright protection will require careful analysis of what is the copyright work in question and the circumstances under which it was created.

Normally the first owner of the copyright work is the person who created it. If it was created by an employee in the course of his or her employment then the first owner will be the employer. In the case of computer-generated works the author is taken to be the person by whom the arrangements necessary for the creation of the work were undertaken. The producer is the 'author' of a sound recording and the producer and principal director the 'authors' of a film. Other specific rules apply in relation to other specific works.

Moral rights

Under special rules in the Act, the author of a copyright literary, dramatic, musical or artistic work and the director of a copyright film have the right to:

- be identified as author;
- object to derogatory treatment of their work;
- prevent a work from being falsely attributed to him as author.

The right to be identified as author has to be asserted and there are various exceptions. Moral rights are generally there to protect what the author sees as their artistic integrity in their creations. The rights can be waived in writing. Moral rights are not assignable. There is a right of action for infringement of moral rights which includes the right to obtain an injunction preventing the infringement continuing.

Similar rights exist under foreign legal systems.

Dealings in copyright work

As with other intellectual property rights, copyright can be assigned. Different rights which might exist in one work (see above) can be assigned to different parties. Copyright can pass under a will and often does so.

Because copyright is so complex and all-pervading, collection societies (such as the Performing Right Society) have grown up which administer copyrights on behalf of individual authors or owners of copyright who assign their rights to collect royalties, for example those involved in the music and newspaper industry. Collection societies will often approach businesses alleging infringement of one kind or another. Take advice when this happens to ensure that you know the extent of any liability. It might be appropriate depending on the nature of one's business to check whether a licence should be obtained.

Prospective copyright, that is rights which are not yet created, is often assigned by the creator. So a contract may provide that an external designer is retained to create some visuals and text for an advertising campaign, the copyright of which will be owned by the commissioning party.

In contrast to design right and save where created in the course of employment, the general rule is that the first owner of a commissioned copyright work is the author. It is always sensible to consider what copyright (or other intellectual property rights) might be created during the course of a commission and ensure that these rights are vested in your company.

As mentioned in Chapter 3, different types of licence can be granted, including non-exclusive, exclusive or sole.

Assignments must be in writing and signed by or on behalf of the assignor to be effective.

Copyright is often jointly owned. This may arise because it is jointly created or because subsequent transactions have created two owners. As opposed to patents, joint owners need permission from each other to use the copyright.

Infringement of copyright

In contrast to other intellectual property rights, the key to copyright infringement is copying. In the example given above in relation to creation, it will be seen that two copyright works came to be independently created. Fundamental to both creation and infringement is the concept of copying. So long as work is 'not copied' then it can qualify as being original, even if the same as someone else's work. An author has the right to prevent another from copying, but cannot complain of independent creation of the same work.

However, copying can be direct or indirect. If the copyright work itself was not copied it could have been copied by reproducing something derived from it, so that copyright in a house plan can be copied by somebody who has never seen it and reproduces from a plan the three-dimensional house on which it is based. Copying can be subconscious. In this sense no 'fault' is necessary but the act of copying has still taken place. In plagiarism cases those accused often assert they did not deliberately copy another author's work, but if it was nevertheless derived from that other author copying has occurred.

What has to be copied for infringement is a 'substantial part' and what is a substantial part will depend entirely on the circumstances. Substance might be related to the originality of what has been taken. A key or famous passage in this way gets more 'protection' than something with little originality in it.

What copyright protects is not the *idea* in the work but the *expression* of that idea. If another way can be found of expressing what might be regarded as the same concept, copyright does not step in. What is or is not copyright infringement in any particular circumstances is often a very difficult legal question. The law also prevents dealings in infringing copies provided the defendant is on notice as to the copyright. Hence it is always appropriate to claim ownership of copyright in works. The reader will be familiar with the common standard assertion of copyright, namely the line:

'© John Smith 2005'.

This tells the reader that John Smith claims to have created the copyright work in 2005. This is not necessary to *create* copyright but because it puts the reader on notice that copyright is *claimed* by Mr Smith it might help to protect it.

One way of 'trapping' someone engaged in copying a copyright work is the use of deliberate 'seed' material. For example, in a literary work a particular word might be misspelled or a particular comma put in slightly the wrong position and if that is reproduced it would be evidence that the material had been copied. One effective way of doing this applies in relation to databases (see below), namely the use of false (seed) names and addresses. For example, if one published for reference purposes a list of solicitors with a false 'seed' name and address this would, if reproduced, suggest that the whole list had been copied. That would be strong evidence against an assertion that the list was independently created, and the material derived by independent work and therefore not copied. Software can similarly be protected by electronic watermarking or the insertion of redundant code. Recently, technology enabling the digital watermarking of soundtracks has also been developed.

As mentioned above in addition to liability for primary or direct infringement a defendant can be liable for dealing in infringing copies. This will include importing, possessing and dealing in infringing copies etc., and applies where the defendant knows or has reason to believe he is dealing in an infringing copy.

There are various exceptions that may apply, such as fair dealing (for example for the purposes of research or private study or the reporting of current events).

Databases

A database is an arranged collection of material which can be accessed and analysed. It is usually electronic. For example, a list of all the solicitors in the United Kingdom and their addresses would constitute a database. Although copyright can subsist in a database as a copyright literary work, special EU-derived regulations apply in relation to databases.

These give a copyright-style property right called a 'database right' which applies specifically to databases that are a product of 'substantial investment'. The owner of the database right (initially the maker) has the right to prevent infringement, which occurs when the data or a substantial part of it is extracted or reutilised without permission. Database right lasts for 15 years. Whether any particular work qualifies for database protection and/or copyright protection is a question of fact in each case.

Passing off

Passing off is a right of action relating to unregistered trade marks and other forms of branding. It is intended to protect against the use of such material in a damaging, unfair or misleading manner.

Unlike most law relating to intellectual property, this right of action is based on common law principles developed over many years and not on statute law. Passing off is similar in many respects to US and European laws protecting unfair trading. Behind all law in this area is a dual purpose:

- to protect the public from being misled as to the trade origin of goods or services; and
- to protect traders from damage to their business by the unfair use of names, symbols or material which are the same as or similar to those of that trader.

Like the law governing registered trade marks, the law of

passing off recognises that many businesses can happily coexist with similar names provided that they are not in the same field of activity. Thus one would not be likely to confuse *Rabbit Books* with *Rabbit Pool Supplies*. The two businesses could happily coexist in the same marketplace. Problems may of course be encountered with the use by two different businesses of the same domain name. In this case, however, provided that the businesses are distinct and are legitimately using their own name there is no true passing off because the customer always knows when it arrives at the address if a mistake has been made.

As will be appreciated from the last paragraph the key to passing off is *confusion*. Is the use of the similar name, product packaging or brand promotion likely to lead customers or potential customers of the claimant to believe that the defendant's goods are those of the claimant? Many potential claims for passing off fail because although the claimant can put together a good argument on other points he will fail to establish confusion or likely confusion.

Elements of passing off

What is required for passing off is a misrepresentation (by a trader), leading to (customer) confusion and (actual or likely) damage. This is best illustrated by example.

Say a trader, Wif Limited, establishes in the UK a reputation in relation to his products, plastic oranges filled with orange juice. He sells many millions of them over many years. The public come to know his goods. They have a high degree of recognition, and although the idea of selling orange juice in an orange shaped container might sound commonplace, nevertheless the public recognise his goods when seeing such a container. They pay little attention to the name of the goods – it is the plastic orange that they see, recognise and buy.

Now a rival introduces an orange-shaped container. He brands it differently. He sells it through the same outlets, but the primary branding – what makes people recognise it – is the shape of the package, the plastic orange.

Lawyers will recognise this example as following the famous *Jif Lemon* case, in which the House of Lords held that there was passing off on similar facts relating to a plastic lemon.

What does this case demonstrate as the elements for passing off? In this example, the misrepresentation was the use of a similar trading indicium (an orange-shaped receptacle), but it might just as easily have been (and usually is) the product name. The key question is whether it is a trade symbol that the buyer recognises, and here the plastic orange, commonplace as it might sound, had for years built up a reputation as the public 'name' of the goods, in the same way as 'a Kodak' means 'a camera made by Kodak'.

Confusion (or the likelihood of confusion) is the second key element. This means 'customer confusion': will customers (or potential customers) of the claimant think that the goods are those of the claimant? Usually the similarity of the product name will be what the claimant is complaining about. But in this case the plastic orange itself, the very receptacle in which the goods were sold, was so recognisable that the use of a similar one led to confusion among customers as to the origin of the goods.

Finally there is damage. This is the *result* of the confusion. It might be lost revenue, lost exclusivity or the potential of lost licensing revenue. There is no need to establish actual loss, just the likelihood of this occurring, and quite often actual loss is not established.

Examples of passing off claims that have failed

In one case the world-famous department store Harrods sued the Harrodian School for passing off. Although it was held that the public might think that the store had sponsored or given support to the school, this was not a sufficient connection. What was needed was confusion as to a real linkage between the two businesses.

In one of two examples given here from the newspaper world, *The European* newspaper sued another publication which was using the title *European Voice*. The claim failed because of lack of evidence of confusion. It was important that the main element in common, the word 'European', was something which should be free for use by all unless some other trade symbols or words of the claimant were used. In another case an interim injunction application by the *Financial Times* against a London daily for passing off based on the use of pink pages for its financial section failed. Although the use of this colour in relation to a financial newspaper by the claimant was well known, there was insufficient evidence of confusion or potential confusion arising from the defendant's adoption of the same colour.

Examples of passing off claims that have succeeded

There have been a whole series of cases over the years involving drinks manufacturers, most famously the Champagne cases, where the joint owners of a reputation in a product name have been able to stop competitors from free-riding on that reputation by the use of different but reminiscent names, such as 'Spanish Champagne'. In these cases the courts have accepted that the champagne producers, and others such as the Scotch whisky producers have a shared reputation and goodwill, depending in large part on their geographical location, which they are able to protect using the law of passing off.

In one famous case involving domain names, in which one of the authors was actually involved as a lawyer, the defendants registered a series of well-known domain names such as marksandspencer.com and bt.com. There was no evidence that the defendants themselves intended to pass off by trading in the same line of business, but it was found that the mere registration and holding of these domain names was threatened passing off because the names themselves were what the court called 'instruments of deception' in the hands of anyone other than their rightful owners. The law could intervene and order their transfer. This case is relatively recent and, while the actual decision has attracted some criticism, demonstrates that the boundaries of this area of the law can extend to different fact situations.

Other claims to protect against unfair trading

In addition to passing off, there are a number of other civil and criminal remedies for or relating to unfair or misleading trading. A detailed analysis is beyond the scope of this work and the reader should consult a solicitor for further information. Some of these include:

- offences regulating seizure and detention of imported goods which are alleged to infringe IP rights;
- Trade Descriptions Act offences, prosecuted by trading standards officers;
- trade libel or malicious falsehood;

- breach of the criminal provisions of the copyright and trade marks laws outlawing criminal activities (for example video piracy);
- breach of the various regulatory and statutory provisions relating to misleading or deceptive advertising.

Domain names

As we have emphasised elsewhere in this book, the Internet is now a vital tool. There is hardly a business in the United Kingdom which does not have a website, which very often functions in the same way as the 'shop front' of the physical trading address of the company. Domain name registration is now sometimes seen as more important than trade mark registration. Although in many ways domain names and trade marks operate in the same way, the registration systems and the systems for enforcing ownership and dealing with dispute resolution are very different.

Computers communicate with each other through addresses called 'IP addresses'. These addresses are numerical. The function of the domain name system is to map easily remembered domain names such as hewitsons.com into numerical IP addresses. Communication between computers takes place through a network, the most important of which is the Worldwide Web, or www.

The first part of a domain name will normally be the name of the company or business concerned (e.g. 'hewitsons') followed by a recognised Internet suffix, for example, .com which designates commercial organisations, .org which designates a non-profit organisation or .net which designates network-related organisations. Others have been created over recent years, for example .bus, .pro and .info.)

Intellectual Property

At the end of the domain name may be a country code such as .uk (United Kingdom), .it (Italy) or .au (Australia). There are also some generic Internet suffixes. The .com, .net and .org domains do not have a country code. The most popular domain names for businesses in the UK are .co.uk and .com. Speaking generally, organisations with an international dimension often prefer the .com as designating business in more than one country. The last part of the domain name will indicate the relevant countries, and for each country there is a body regulating the use of the names. In the UK it is Nominet (*http://www.nominet.org.uk*).

Domain names are unique. While trade marks are divided into particular classes and there can be a number of identical trade marks with different owners in different classes, there can only be one hewitsons.com in the system. It is therefore vitally important that an appropriate domain name is selected and reserved, or purchased, right at the beginning of a business's life. Without an appropriate domain name the business may be hampered or appear less than professional. On the other hand, domain name registries do not reject applications for registration based on the rights of existing domain name owners. That is not their function. Hence a slightly different spelling, the insertion of a dash or some other minor adjustment to a name can result in it being registered. This can lead to disputes. Sometimes as well as registering the name of a company it is advisable to register flagship product names or names similar to that of the company in order to avoid others claiming them. Domain name registration is generally not very expensive and it is often money well spent.

A company will usually retain a website design and host company to help design and maintain its website, and that company often provides hosting services for the domain name or names of the company. It is important to have in place effective systems for renewal. Domain names need to be renewed regularly otherwise they lapse and can be obtained by a competitor or one of the many businesses that operate by collecting and selling unregistered domain names.

As mentioned above, domain name disputes can be dealt with in different ways from other intellectual property disputes. Nominet and other registrars have dispute resolution procedures to deal with disputes about ownership or the use of any particular domain names. However, it may be appropriate, for example if speed is needed, to apply to the court in any particular country for appropriate orders. The necessary course in any particular circumstances depends on the facts. Where the domain name corresponds to a brand name or trade mark and has been acquired by a 'cybersquatter' in the hope of making a big profit by selling it to the brand holder, the domain name registrars and the courts have little sympathy and will normally order the transfer of the domain name to the rightful owner. This does normally involve expense and uncertainty which can be avoided by acquiring the relevant domain name before launching the product.

Often a company has to negotiate the purchase of a domain name from a business that may own it and not wish to use it any more or from some operator who has legitimately registered a number of domain names and then wishes to sell them. The tactics to be adopted in negotiation will depend on the name, its value and with whom one is dealing. Escrow services are provided by some businesses for these transactions.

More information

- Nominet (*http://www.nominet.org.uk/*) runs all .uk

domain names and their website has a host of information about the domain name registration process.

- ICANN (Internet Corporation for Assigned Names and Mumbers) (*http://www.icann.org/*) is a US non-profit organisation that looks after the Internet's infrastructure. Its Uniform Domain-Name Dispute-Resolution Policy (*http://www.icann.org/udrp/udrp.htm*) is used by all registrars who deal with generic names such as .com and .net.

Confidential information and know-how

Confidential information and know-how are not intellectual property rights in the traditional sense, but are often nevertheless just as important to a company's business and its value, and just as necessary to protect as a patent, a design or a trade mark.

Confidential information is secret, valuable information protectable by means of agreement or obligation. If someone to whom the information is given discloses it on terms breaching the agreement or obligation, that will entitle a claim to be made for damages arising.

Know-how is not necessarily secret, although it can be. Know-how is just that, some piece of industry knowledge or skill capable of reproduction in some form, which is of value to a business. If it is not a secret, know-how is harder to protect. It can be protected by imposing a contractual obligation on a party to whom it is disclosed not to use it for other purposes, but because it is publicly known, it is often difficult to show that there has been an abuse of an undertaking not to use know-how. Nevertheless agreements for licensing or sale of know-how are common and often know-how is the most valuable part of a company's business.

Why is confidential information important?

As mentioned above, some intellectual property rights need to be a secret before the application for registration is made. Keeping a new idea secret might be key to a patentable invention. If a procedure or process is not protectable by means of a patent or a design, it may be protectable by using an obligation of confidence on those who are given the information.

Companies are often approached by people without the resources or skills to develop a particular process or product they have devised. A properly drafted confidentiality agreement will allow the disclosure of that information to the company on terms which allow its development and the proper remuneration of the party whose idea it was. Until such an agreement is in place a developer may well be reluctant without good reason to disclose it to the company without any means of protection. On the other hand, until the company sees it, it will not know whether it is worth putting resources into. Confidentiality agreements can help here.

Ways in which confidential information is protected

Employees have a general duty of good faith to their employer, and it may be appropriate, for example in the case of specific employees who have a particular need to know certain information, to have specific confidentiality obligations in their contracts of employment. General know-how acquired by an employee during the course of his employment is not protectable as confidential, but specific information about key company products, such as that contained in chemical formulae, usually is.

A company ought to have in place rules and procedures for handling the confidential information of other parties which the company deals with, and for its disclosure to other companies in certain circumstances. Often the information will need to be marked in some way and the number of copies which can be kept restricted. It may be appropriate if information is being disclosed to a joint venture partner for that information to only be disclosed to those who have a 'need to know' the information in order to achieve the aim. Whatever is done, it is necessary to ensure that the process is controlled. Once confidential information leaks out it is difficult, often impossible, to recapture its value. Generally once disclosure is made by the company itself or without the fault of anyone it is difficult to remedy.

Confidentiality agreements

To achieve all these aims companies routinely enter into standard form confidentiality agreements. Your lawyer will be able to produce such an agreement tailored to meet the specific needs of any given circumstance. These are dealt with in detail in Chapter 3. Generally such agreements will need to:

- identify the information;
- detail to whom it has been disclosed;
- make provision about the making of copies and their return;

- set out in what circumstances the information can be disclosed (for example if required by law);
- deal with the return of confidential information at the end of the term of the agreement;
- provide remedies in case of breach of any of the obligations in the agreement.

Just what is necessary in any particular case is a matter for individual tailoring. It is vital to ensure that information which is the subject of a confidentiality obligation or undertaking is properly defined and identified.

Supplementary protection certificates

Once a patent for an invention has been granted, it will run for 20 years from the date of the original application. However, in the case of new drugs and certain agrochemicals, the product may only come onto the market with a few years of the patent left to run because of the length of time needed to complete both the development cycle and clinical or field trials. In order to have the originator compensated for the extra time it takes to bring these products to market, a degree of extension of protection for patented pharmaceuticals and agrochemicals has been introduced in Europe, comparable to that already available in the US and Japan. The supplementary protection certificate (SPC) provides limited protection after the patent has expired for patented medicinal or agrochemical products which have been authorised for human use.

The extra time gained by an SPC depends on the length of time between filing the patent application and the authorisation of the product. The minimum delay before an SPC can be granted is six years, which will give rise to a one-year SPC. The extension then accrues annually, up to a maximum extension of five years, granted after a delay of ten or more years.

The protection granted is not as broad as that of the original patent. The SPC will only cover the product for which the licence is held and its use as a medicinal or agrochemical product. New formulations will not be included, although protection may be extended to a licensed product which is an ester or salt of a patented acid.

In the case of many novel drugs, a licensee undertakes the clinical trials which have led to the market authorisation. However, the patent holder rather than the licensee must apply for the SPC, but he will need the marketing authorisation to do so. The licence agreement should therefore oblige the licensee to supply it to him for this purpose. This application must be completed within six months of the date of authorisation or six months of the date of grant, whichever is later. Unless the agreement clearly states otherwise, a licence which continues for the duration of the patent will bind both parties throughout the term of the SPC.

An SPC gives protection against any of the actions that would infringe the original patent (making, using or selling the protected compound). However, recent changes in the law mean that copies of the original branded compound may be tested during the term of the SPC in order to allow their registration as soon as the SPC has expired.

Data exclusivity

Protection of drugs that have been granted licensing approval does not necessarily end with the expiry of the SPC. There are also rights associated with the data generated by clinical trials which are important to the originator of the drug. Under current law, certain details of the clinical trial must be entered into a European clinical trials database, and there are proposals that all clinical trials data should be publicly available from one year after market authorisation. However, these and other publicly available data cannot be used by competitors such as generic drug companies until a certain amount of time has passed.

Generic drug companies usually gain marketing authorisation for their products by demonstrating that the drug has the same active composition as an approved patented drug, or that it has the same clinical effect, which is again usually determined by reference to the data relating to the original product. The generics companies are therefore able to bring products to market using data generated by the patent holder or licensee, and consequently have very low development costs.

However, competitors cannot rely on clinical data from the originator to support their own product licence application until the product has been authorised for eight years. A further two years must then elapse before the generic drug can be placed on the market, giving a total of ten year's data exclusivity. An additional year's protection can be obtained if there is a significant new use for the drug.

In practice, this means that if marketing authorisation has been delayed until close to the end of the patent term, any potential entrant to the market cannot rely on the originators' clinical data to obtain a product licence for up to eleven years. This exclusivity may therefore last for up to six years after the SPC has expired. Although not actually extending patent protection, the requirement for a competitor to do its own testing makes a barrier for the entry of generic drugs onto the market.

Semiconductor topography rights

Special intellectual property rights have been introduced to protect the shape or layout of multi-layer semiconductors since the investment in designing the topography of microchips is very high. Protection originated in the USA, where the legislation stipulates that only those countries whose governments have introduced reciprocal legislation are entitled to protection of their topographies in the USA. Accordingly, in 1989, a specialised type of unregistered design right was incorporated into the Copyright, Designs and Patents Act 1988 by the Semiconductor Products (Protection of Topography) Regulations 1989. This right arises automatically in the UK once the design has been recorded in a design document, but it needs to be registered in most other countries where it exists.

The protection is restricted to the particular shape or layout designed by the right owner. This means the pattern fixed, or intended to be fixed, in or upon a layer of a semiconductor product, or a layer of material in the course of and for the purpose of the manufacture of a semiconductor product. Additionally, the arrangement of the patterns fixed, or intended to be fixed, in or upon the layers of a semiconductor product in relation to one another is also protected. A 'semiconductor product' is defined as one which performs an electronic function and which consists of two or more layers, at least one of which is composed of semiconducting material and in or upon one or more of which is fixed a pattern appertaining to that or another function. To qualify for protection, the design must only 'not be commonplace in the design field'. A rearrangement of commonplace elements provides sufficient originality.

This right is infringed by either making an object to the design or by making a design document for the purpose of manufacturing a copy of all or a substantial part of the semiconductor product. However, if the design is reproduced privately for non-commercial use, there is a defence to an infringement claim. More importantly, reproducing the topography of the chip in order to analyse it is also allowed. A new chip may be built as a result of this evaluation so that, for this design right, reverse engineering is permitted. The test for infringement is how much additional, original work has been done by the alleged infringer. This test differs from copyright in that infringement is not an issue of how much of the old can be traced in the new.

Ownership of this right is granted to the commissioner or employer of the design, or in the absence of such a person, its creator.

The topography is protected for 15 years from the end of the year in which the design was first recorded, or for ten years from the end of the year in which articles made to the design were first made available for sale or hire. These periods can be cumulative for chip designs, a distinction between chips and other designs. The theoretical maximum duration is therefore nearly 26 years. Unlike the provisions for other, non-chip designs, there is no requirement for licences of right in the last five years of the right.

Remedies

There are a number of common elements in relation to the remedies granted for infringement of intellectual property rights. In most cases it is not necessary to establish that the infringement has been intentional in any sense but in some cases the absence of necessary knowledge means damages are not payable. This is one reason that notice of ownership or claimed ownership, e.g. ™ trade mark, ® patent (with details and number) or © copyright, often appear on or in relation to works or items the subject of claimed rights. Take specific advice on this, so that an incomplete or incorrect symbol is not used in any particular case.

Once a registered or unregistered right has been infringed, the claimant has a right to prevent by court action that conduct from continuing.

Somebody complaining of infringement of intellectual property rights will be looking for the following sorts of remedy. These are explained a little more fully in context in Chapter 5 on dispute resolution (see below), but are worth flagging up now:

- an injunction or agreement preventing the infringing conduct;
- costs and damages;
- information concerning the infringer and the source of the infringing items;
- delivery up of any infringing items or destruction of them so that the problem cannot reoccur.

Quite often in intellectual property cases the primary aim is not to recover damages for infringement of the rights but rather to prevent the damaging conduct from continuing. If proceedings are taken against a retailer the key is often to establish where the infringing goods came from and follow the trail back to the manufacturer. If a claim for damages is made, the claimant, if it succeeds, will usually have an option as to whether to seek damages or an account of profits. Damages are to put the injured party back into the position it was before the infringement took place and often take the form of a notional royalty for the infringement, while an account of profits is an adding up of the profits made by the infringer, less the overheads and other costs of making those profits.

Other issues

Normally intellectual property actions must be brought within six years of the time the cause of action arose. This will apply in relation to each separate act of infringement. It is open to a defendant to assert that the claimant is 'estopped' from bringing a claim because of acquiescence or delay in enforcing the right. Time limits generally and whether any of these rules apply in any particular circumstance are questions for legal advice based on the particular context.

There are provisions in UK legislation and that of other countries relating to threats of proceedings for intellectual property right infringement. These provisions are particularly important for those in business engaged in the day-to-day maintenance and protection of their intellectual property rights. The provisions are complex and there are exceptions, but the thrust of them is that in the case of patents, trade marks (but not service marks) and UK and EU designs (registered and unregistered), someone damaged by a threat of proceedings can bring an action to prevent those threats and recover damages arising from them. This has existed for many years in relation to patents and it was only relatively recently introduced in relation to other rights. The idea behind the rules is to prevent the owner of an intellectual property right from misusing it by issuing threats without justification and damaging the business of other traders. The case law is extremely complex and has been recently made more complex by changes to the Patents Act which provide special rules in relation to patents that do not apply to other intellectual property rights.

Intellectual Property

The lesson for businesses is to be aware that assertions of or threats relating to intellectual property rights can result in claims against the maker and to always seek legal advice before making any such assertions.

3

Dealing in IP rights

Overview

Since IP rights are assets they can be made the subject of commercial dealings, i.e. made available by the owner to others in various ways. Some IP transactions (such as the assignment of patents and trade marks) must be in writing to be valid. However, it is advisable to make sure that any IP contract entered into is recorded in writing as each party's rights and obligations can then be set out in black and white. In the absence of a written agreement, it is much harder to work out who is meant to do what and who is entitled to what, which can be particularly problematic if a dispute arises. The parties may have agreed on these issues once but if a dispute looms, people tend to develop selective memories!

For a contract to be legally binding each party must promise to give something to the other. This usually means paying money in exchange for performing an obligation. In the absence of this, the agreement should be in the form of a deed, which is worded slightly differently and has different requirements for signature. You should seek advice from a lawyer on whether a contract or deed is appropriate and, unless you are very experienced, always involve your lawyer in the drafting and negotiation of your IP agreement.

We now move on to the different types of IP agreement which you may encounter.

Assignments

An assignment is essentially a transfer of ownership of the IP rights in question from one party to another. The assignor gives its rights up and ownership passes to the assignee in the same way that one might sell, say, a house or a car.

The following are some of the more important points which should be noted in connection with the transfer of IP rights:

- Only the registered proprietor of a patent or the registered exclusive licensee may initiate proceedings against an infringer, so once the patent rights have passed to the assignee it should register the fact at the Patent Office. Your patent attorney can do this for you.

- As with patents, the assignee of a registered trade mark must register the fact.

- The goodwill of a business (defined below) generally accompanies the trade marks. If the trade marks are to be assigned without the associated goodwill, therefore, this must be made clear in the agreements effecting the assignment.

- The assignment of a registered design must expressly include any related unregistered design right but, conversely, the assignment of an unregistered design right will automatically include any associated registered design.

'Goodwill' is the term used in this context to summarise the intangible value of the company's name or reputation.

Assignees of patents, designs and trade marks should ensure that their ownership is registered at the Patent Office or other appropriate registry. Your lawyer or patent attorney can help with this.

Licences

Under a licence the owner of the IP rights in question retains ownership but permits another party to use them to varying degrees, in other words to do acts which without that permission would be an infringement of those IP rights.

Licences can vary in terms of the scope of the rights granted with respect to:

- duration, i.e. how long the licence lasts;
- territory, i.e. in what countries or regions the licensee may exploit those rights;
- field of use, i.e. what the licensee may do with the IP rights in question. For example, a licensee may be entitled to use any software covered by the licence for internal research rather than commercial purposes. Taking another example, the licensee may be entitled to use a patent to make and sell a drug but only for use in the human rather than the veterinary field. If the IP has only one application, field may not be an issue.

Furthermore, the licence may be exclusive, sole or non-exclusive. Under an exclusive licence, no one other than the licensee can exercise the rights in question in the nominated field and territory, not even the licensor. Under a sole licence, only the licensor and licensee may exercise those rights. Under a non-exclusive licence, the licensor may appoint as many licensees of the rights as it likes and itself exercise the licensed rights. Obviously, the licensee is going to prefer to have exclusivity as then it won't be competing with anybody but will always have to pay more for this. Exclusive patent licensees are also permitted to take action against infringers as if they owned that IP. However, they should register their exclusivity at the Patent Office in order to be able to assert this right. Again, your patent attorney or lawyer can help with this.

All IP contracts will contain elements of assignment and/or licensing. We now deal with the most common types of IP contracts which you are likely to encounter, their purpose and the provisions which they are likely to contain. One general point worth making is that the intellectual property rights which are the subject of the contract should always be detailed as precisely as possible, preferably in a schedule at the back. Otherwise there could be ambiguity as to precisely what is being transferred or licensed. Registered rights can be summarised by reference to registered numbers and the date upon which the right was granted. A more nebulous right such as know-how might have to be summarised by reference to specific reports, plans, drawings or computer files.

The most common types of contract which a business will enter into in respect of its intellectual property are discussed in following sections.

Confidentiality agreements

Before entering into a full-form agreement, of whatever nature, the parties may wish to exchange confidential information so that each party can judge what the other has to offer. Such information may pertain to the disclosing party's technology, commercial operations, business contacts or financial or accounting status. However, the disclosing party will certainly not want that information passed on by the other party without its permission. If such information were to get into the hands of one of the disclosing party's competitors, untold damage could be done.

Under English law, a recipient has an implied obligation not to divulge information disclosed to it under circumstances of confidentiality. However, it is far better to strengthen this position by relying on an express and written confidentiality agreement, detailing the information being disclosed, the purpose of the disclosure (such as the parties using it to decide whether to enter into a further agreement) and the period for which it must be kept confidential. The agreement should also make it clear whether only one party will be disclosing confidential information or whether the parties will be exchanging it.

The agreement should also specify what categories of information will not be viewed as subject to the obligation of non-disclosure, for example information in the public domain, information which the recipient is required to disclose by law, and information received or generated by the recipient independently without reliance on the disclosures made by the other party under the confidentiality agreement.

It is worth bearing in mind that if you disclose sensitive information about your business to another party which then lets it leak out, the damage will be done and it is difficult to put the genie back in the bottle. You might get an injunction to prevent the other side from making further disclosures and successfully sue for damages, but none of this may compensate for the harm done. The best way of minimising the risk of this happening is only to disclose confidential information to the other side to the extent that it is absolutely necessary to do so. Admittedly, there is a delicate balance to be struck here, because the more you disclose about your technology and commercial potential, the more likely you are to persuade the other side to enter into a contract with you.

Another practical point to consider is that if you are disclosing the same information to a number of potential partners, and one of them passes that information on without authorisation, it may be difficult to identify who the culprit is. You have a better chance of doing so if you keep a careful record of precisely what was disclosed to whom, when and for what purpose. Furthermore, as has been suggested above to protect against copyright infringement, electronic disclosures can be 'watermarked' to ensure traceability.

Confidentiality is important even if the value of your business's intellectual property primarily resides in patents. A competitor may not be able to infringe your patents with impunity, but if it gets its hands on related confidential information, it may be able to come up with a way of working round those patents, thereby enabling it to come up with competing technology, outside the 'ring fence', which can be used to your business's detriment without treading on your rights.

All the agreements detailed below will also need to contain confidentiality clauses addressing all these issues, since they almost always entail the disclosure of sensitive information.

Materials transfer agreements

As well as disclosing its confidential information, a company may make samples of its technology available to the other side for evaluation, to aid the other side in deciding whether to enter into a contract to buy, exploit or develop that technology. Such arrangements should also be the subject of an express written agreement which should clearly define the purpose for which the technology is being made available and restrict the recipient's use to that purpose. Furthermore, in evaluating the technology the recipient may come up with ideas or improvements of its own and the agreement should specify who will own or have access to these. Ideally, the party disclosing the original technology will want to own these but the recipient party may feel that this is unjustified since its effort has produced the improvements in question or may only agree if money changes hands. A common compromise reached is for the parties to agree that any improvements developed by the recipient will not be used unless the parties enter into a further agreement which will govern their ownership and use.

Finally, since the materials transfer governs the supply and testing of physical material, such as a prototype device or chemical compound, the agreement will have to deal with:

- who is responsible for its delivery to the evaluating party and its return at the end of the tests;
- any legal or regulatory requirements in connection with its transport, storage or use;
- the obligation on the transferor to supply any information available to it on the use, safe handling and toxicity (if appropriate) of the materials;
- any specific protocols which must be used in the conduct of the tests so that, for example, the material is not damaged.

If biological or chemical materials are being tested, then extra materials may be grown or synthesised during the tests. If so, the transferor will want these materials destroyed or returned as well.

Heads of agreement

These are often also known as letters of intent or heads of terms. Heads of agreement summarise the provisions of the full-form agreement which the parties envisage entering into. They are often relied upon in the early stages of negotiations for licensing and collaboration deals, enabling the parties to thrash out the basic principles of the deal early on which can then get fleshed out later in detailed negotiations, with input from lawyers and other professional advisers.

Under English law, these sorts of agreements are non-binding, so that even if the parties sign up to them the contractual terms are still up for grabs and the parties are subsequently free to negotiate completely different terms if they wish. Alternatively, they do not have to enter into any agreement at all, whatever the heads of agreement envisaged. However, in some countries such as the USA, heads of agreement are binding, so that the parties are construed as being obliged to enter into an agreement along the lines reflected in the heads of agreement. To avoid any misunderstanding, especially when the parties are from different countries, it is always best therefore to put 'Non-binding; subject to contract' at the top of heads of agreement if you do not wish them to be binding.

Some businesses make the mistake of spending an inordinate amount of time negotiating and perfecting the heads of agreement and then going through exactly the same hoops when drawing up and finalising the full-form contract. This can effectively double the negotiating time, leading to costly delays. Accordingly, it is usually best just to use heads of agreement to encapsulate the broad principles and then move to negotiation of the full-form contract as soon as possible. If both parties have a clear idea of the bare bones of the contract from the outset, then summarising them in heads of terms may really not be necessary at all and the parties may be able to proceed immediately to negotiating the full agreement.

A final point worth noting is that if the parties sign heads of agreement and never sign a full-form contract but nevertheless start performing their respective obligations under the arrangement, in the event of a dispute the court may use those heads of agreement as evidence of who was meant to do what. This is another reason why they should be used with caution.

Options

Often a company may grant another company an option to decide whether to enter into a licence or some other further agreement with it. Such agreements should always be in writing. Furthermore, it should always be very clear:

- whether the option is exclusive or non-exclusive, i.e. whether during that period the licensor is free to offer similar rights to other parties or not;

- which technology the option covers and the nature of the rights on offer;

- how long the option will last for, i.e how long the period is within which the potential licensee may exercise the option before its right to do so expires. From the licensor's point of view, this period should always be finite; otherwise there is a danger of the option subsisting forever and the licensor being hampered in its freedom to license the technology elsewhere. In any event, so there is no ambiguity, the potential licensee should always be obliged to exercise the option in writing;

- if the licensee wishes to exercise the option, how long the parties have to negotiate the full-form agreement. Again, from the licensor's point of view, there should always be a finite period within which they must finalise and sign the formal agreement, after which, if agreement has not been reached, all bets are off. Otherwise, there is a danger, if negotiations drag on or go quiet, of the licensor assuming that the option has expired and it can now take the technology elsewhere, and the licensee assuming that its rights are still subsisting and alleging a breach if the licensor then enters into an agreement with a third party.

Manufacturing agreements

Often the companies which develop products do not have the expertise or resources to manufacture them themselves and will therefore subcontract this role out to a manufacturer. In such circumstances, the manufacturer will need to be granted a licence of the first company's intellectual property in order to manufacture products for it. The licensor company will want the agreement to make it clear that the licensee manufacturer may only use the intellectual property to manufacture products for the licensor or its nominees. It may also wish to impose quality control measures such as:

- restricting the manufacturer from subcontracting its obligations without the licensor's prior written consent; and

- the requirement that the manufacturer comply with all the licensor's instructions regarding branding; and

- the requirement that the manufacturer manufacture in compliance with an agreed specification and any relevant regulatory requirements; and

- the right of the licensor to inspect the manufacturer's manufacturing process and facilities; and

- detailed procedures and remedies which will kick in if any products manufactured turn out to be defective. In such circumstances, the licensor will either want to be reimbursed the price paid or have the products in question replaced free of charge. Furthermore, if it sells defective products on to customers and incurs liability to those customers as a result, then it will want an indemnity from the manufacturer, i.e. an obligation on the manufacturer to 'foot the bill' for whatever the licensor must do or pay to compensate that customer. In such circumstances the licensor would also want the manufacturer to take out product liability insurance so that meeting this obligation can be paid for. If the parties disagree on whether a product is defective or not or whose fault the defect is, then the agreement can provide for the issue to be referred to an independent expert.

The licensor will also want guarantees in the contract that the manufacturer can produce the required levels of products to meet the licensor's and its customers' demands.

Often, as well as being required to manufacture the licensor's products, the manufacturer is required to develop a scaled-up process so that those products can be produced in large commercial volumes economically and efficiently. In such circumstances, intellectual property rights may well reside in the process developed, certainly in the form of know-how, which may even be patentable. As this process directly relates to its products the licensor will want to own it. Failing that, it should at least have access to it so that if necessary it can use that process itself or appoint other manufacturers to use it in the future, since otherwise it cannot cut loose from the first manufacturer, even if it becomes technically or commercially desirable to so. However, the original manufacturer may also want to reserve the right to use that process in the scaled-up manufacture for its other customers. If those other customers are competitors of the first customer, that could be a problem. Who owns and who has access to any manufacturing process developed is therefore of paramount importance and must be agreed and expressly tackled in the contract.

Research agreements

The company may have developed its intellectual property in-house. However, it may not necessarily have the expertise and facilities to do this, or it may not wish to incur the extra liability which acquiring employees and facilities to generate its core technology would entail. Often, therefore, companies pay for research to be carried out by another party, on the understanding that the results of that research will be made available to the company. Outsourcing research also enables the company to pick and choose from the best researchers worldwide in any given field.

Often the party contracted to carry out the research is a university or some other academic institution. However, since in many respects universities have different mindsets and agendas from commercial companies, negotiations between the two can be problematic. For example, companies, particularly if under pressure from investors, licensees and customers, will wish to negotiate and conclude the contract quickly but many universities are still under-resourced in terms of experienced contract officers and this can slow the process up. Furthermore, universities and individual academics set great store by publications, but companies wish to protect the commercial viability of technology by keeping it confidential and applying for patents, so publication is often the last thing which they want. These problems and others were identified in the Treasury-sponsored Lambert Review of December 2003, which explored in depth the state of business–university collaboration in the UK and the extent to which the different aims and priorities of each can hamper the effective development and commercialisation of research.

In this context, the research agreement between the company and the university (or any other research body for that matter) should contain the following elements:

- *A full description of the project envisaged*, if possible divided into project stages and milestones so that performance can be measured. If the company is paying in stages, then it would want the right to withhold any of those payments if the corresponding milestones had not been reached on time. This will give the university an incentive to carry out the research promptly and diligently. On the other hand, the university may require an acknowledgement from the company that the research is exploratory in nature and that the university cannot therefore guarantee its success or that a viable commercial product or process will come out of it.

- *How the university will be paid*. The company may merely wish to pay a fixed fee or staged payments for the conduct of the research. The university, on the other hand, may instead or in addition want shares or share options in the company or royalties based on a percentage of revenue derived from the future exploitation of any technology which comes out of the research. The company may be reluctant to agree to this since it cannot immediately quantify what it will be paying. However, universities are increasingly demanding such open-ended and long-term remuneration. If the university agrees to a royalty, then the company may insist that the percentage be low if the research in question is at an early stage and will require much further development and significant input from other parties before a viable product or process capable of commercial exploitation is reached.

- *It may be vital that the research is carried out by a particular department or group of individuals.* Indeed, the research may hinge on the involvement of a particular project leader. If that project leader leaves and is not replaced by another of equivalent qualifications or experience within a set period, then the company may want the right to terminate the project.

- *The company will want to own the intellectual property contained in the results of the research.* If those results are to comprise the company's core technology then ownership may be vital; otherwise it might be difficult for the company to attract investors. However, increasingly universities are only willing to grant exclusive licences of the results and sometimes these licences are restricted to the company's particular field of operation. This is less desirable from the company's point of view because the university may therefore have the ability to terminate the licence and claw back its rights if, for example, the company has not exploited that technology within a set period which may have been decided fairly arbitrarily. It may be hard for a realistic time limit to be agreed in advance when neither party knows what technical obstacles may be thrown up or what the market will be like. This puts pressure on the company, and often it may not do the university much good either; even if it terminates the licence, it may have difficulty finding another company capable of exploiting that technology and by the time it does so competing technology may have overtaken it.

- *The university will usually want to retain the right to use the results for internal research and teaching.* In such circumstances, the company should ensure that no confidential information or potentially patentable invention is disclosed and that the research does not stray into work for other commercial sponsors.

- *In order to facilitate its use of the results, the company may also require a licence of the university's background intellectual property,* i.e. intellectual property in the university's possession or control generated independently of the project. If so, the agreement should expressly provide for this. The company will want this licence to be free but the university may want to charge an extra royalty.

- *The university should be expressly precluded from using any other funding on the project without the company's consent.* Otherwise, the university might involve another sponsor who also wants ownership or exploitation rights over the project results and this would encroach upon the rights which the company is after.

- *The company will not want to find that in conducting the project the university has infringed someone else's intellectual property* and will want assurances that it can make full use of the results of the project without infringing any third party's rights. The agreement should therefore contain a warranty by the university to this effect. The university may argue that as an academic institution it does not have time to carry out the extensive patent searches necessary to give such an unqualified warranty. In such circumstances, the university may merely be willing to warrant that the project results do not, to the best of the university's knowledge, infringe any third-party rights.

In the light of the conclusions of the Lambert Review mentioned above, in February 2005 the government launched a new set of web-based guidance notes and model agreement templates, drawn up by a working group chaired by Richard Lambert. These do not intend to affect established strategic relationships between large companies and universities which will have their own procedures in place. Rather, they are intended to help smaller businesses and universities without business links to implement the recommendations of the review by focusing on the major issues of financial contributions, the exploitation of intellectual property and academic publication of the results of the research. There are five agreements for specific situations and a checklist to help decide which agreement is the most appropriate. They have been drafted to represent a reasonable and practical compromise for both parties rather than the best position for either the university or its sponsor. At the time of writing, these agreements can be found at *www.innovation.gov.uk/lambertagreements/*. The first three agreements cover situations where the universities take the lead in directing the research. In these, the university retains rights in the IP and, if the research was undertaken for largely academic reasons, the sponsor may be offered a non-exclusive licence.

However, where the results of the project are likely to be of interest to both parties, the sponsor may negotiate for an exclusive licence. If the sponsor can identify specific results which it needs to own in order to exploit them effectively, it may be granted an assignment.

Where the research has been carried out to address the sponsor's business interests, the sponsor will obtain the right to use the IP and the university will retain the right to use it for non-commercial purposes. The university's right to publish the results may even be restricted in the case of contract research.

Of course, while these agreements inevitably ease the process, they will not solve the other problems such as the fundamental failure to agree on key points and the slow turnaround time which sometimes plague negotiations between academia and industry.

Collaboration agreements

Often two or more parties collaborate in the development of technology because it enables them to pool their expertise and resources, thereby accomplishing more than each of them would in isolation. Sometimes they may wish to collaborate because they specialise in completely different but complementary areas. For example, in the pharmaceutical sector, one party might have developed a drug and the other party a drug delivery device, and the parties may wish to collaborate in the further development and commercialisation of both products combined. Often a collaboration involves a university and a number of industrial sponsors who fund the university to generate technology which they will then all have access to. Such collaborations between industries and academia can often rely on third-party funding from, for example, the Department of Trade and Industry (DTI) and the European Commission. However, applying for such grants can be a time-consuming business and they can have strings attached. For example, failure to perform the project diligently or commercialise the results can result in the funding being clawed back. Sometimes, the grantor may wish to have a licence to use the results also. Consequently, in such circumstances, the parties should always ensure that the collaboration agreement between them does not contradict the terms of any outside grant.

Obviously, the collaboration agreement should detail precisely what the project will entail and what each party will be expected to do, whether in the form of research or funding. The agreement should also accommodate the possibility of any participant dropping out, in which case the question arises of whether the project will be wound up or whether it can continue in the hands of the remaining collaborators. The parties may also wish the agreement to contemplate the inclusion of extra collaborators at a later date. If any party will need access to any of the other parties' intellectual property in order to conduct its part of the project then the agreement should cater for this too. Each party will want the others' rights restricted to using its intellectual property to conduct the project and, if appropriate, to facilitate exploitation of any technology produced.

The thorniest issue to tackle in such agreements is who will own the intellectual property resulting from the collaboration. It may be the case that each party has had a clearly defined role and as a result has produced its own discrete intellectual property. In such circumstances, it would be logical for each party to own its intellectual property with, perhaps, a licence of the other parties' to the extent necessary to facilitate commercialisation. The issue becomes more problematic if any such intellectual property has been generated jointly by any of the collaborators in which case, in the first instance, it will be owned jointly.

Joint ownership of intellectual property can be problematic because of the following:

- In some countries (such as the UK) co-owners of some intellectual property rights cannot automatically grant licences and take infringement action independently of each other whereas in others (such as the US) they can. This can lead to confusion if the intellectual property rights in question, and their owners, reside in more than one country.

- If the parties decide that they will only exploit the intellectual property jointly, then they need to agree on how to allocate revenue derived from exploitation, and responsibility for exploitation, applying for patent protection and defending those patents. If they cannot agree on these things because, for example, one party does not want to contribute to the costs of any patent application or litigation, then the whole collaboration could grind to a halt.

- It would be more clear-cut if only one party owned intellectual property and the other parties accordingly assigned their rights to that party. That party could then be the sole exploiter and pay the other parties royalties. However, in a collaboration of equals, the sole ownership of jointly created intellectual property may be politically unacceptable. The best compromise might be if the other co-owners of the intellectual property exclusively licensed exploitation rights to one party which would then commercialise that intellectual property and pay them royalties.

- As was said above, another alternative may be for each collaborator to be able to exploit the project results independently of the others. However, in those circumstances, they could find they are competing with each other.

Where the project has been conducted by a university on behalf of one or more commercial sponsors, the intellectual property generated by the university will usually be assigned to one or more of the sponsors. However, in such circumstances, the university may want a licence back to use that intellectual property for internal research purposes only (see above).

Commercial licences

Often, the company developing a product or process initially may not have the resources to further develop it. It may have limited or no manufacturing capability and may not have the infrastructure to market, sell and distribute the finished product. Furthermore, the product in question may have to meet various regulatory requirements before it can be marketed as is particularly the case for those sectors in which defective products could be a health hazard. These requirements will not be attainable without a certain level of expertise and resources. For example, pharmaceuticals must have passed clinical trials and have received a marketing authorisation before they can be sold. Similar regulatory hoops exist for other industries.

In such circumstances, the company may grant a licence to another party to use the relevant intellectual property to commercialise the product or process in question. As has already been said, such a licence may be restricted by territory or field of application, and may be exclusive, sole or non-exclusive. The licensor will wish to restrict the licensee to a specific field or territory if it believes there are other more suitable potential licensees in other fields or territories. The licensee, on the other hand, may wish the scope of the licence to be wider so that it has the potential to expand into other fields or territories.

As was said above, many licensees will not be interested unless they get exclusivity. However, in such circumstances it may be reasonable, since the licensor has thrown all its eggs in one basket, for the licensee to be obliged to meet agreed targets in terms of sales and royalties. If it failed to do so the licensor could then terminate the agreement and find another licensee. Without this incentive, there is a danger of the licensee sitting on the technology because it has other priorities or prefers to provide an alternative, competing technology instead, and the licensor not making anything out of it at all.

In the case of some technology, rather than appointing one licensee and charging a lot for the privilege, it is more advantageous for the licensor to make licences available to everybody across the board without anyone having to pay too much. This strategy is more important when the technology in question facilitates the production of the end product instead of being the end product itself. Non-bespoke software and biotech research tools often fall into this category.

The licensor will also need to consider how it will be paid for the granting of the licence. There are a number of options, namely:

- *An upfront payment in the form of a lump sum paid on the granting of the licence.* This is advantageous from the licensor's point of view in that it gives the licensor a financial return immediately. On the other hand, if the licensee subsequently makes a lot of money out of exploiting the intellectual property in question without being obliged to make any further payments to the licensor, the licensor may be short changed. For this reason, the licensee may be the one wanting merely to pay an initial lump sum. On the other hand, this could financially squeeze the licensee if it has to pay the licensor before it itself has made any money out of the technology licensed.

Intellectual Property

- *Milestone payments due on the attainment of a specific event*, e.g. the granting of marketing authorisation from a relevant regulatory authority in a key territory or the first commercial sale. From the licensor's point of view this gives it the chance of receiving further payments in the future, subject to those milestones being met, of course. Again, however, the licensee could be put under financial pressure as a result since it may have paid money to obtain a given milestone (for example, by further developing the technology, conducting a trial or meeting regulatory requirements) and it will then have to pay even more money to the licensor, all before it has started making money from the technology itself.

- *Royalties based on a percentage of sales revenue.* This enables the licensor to benefit from the licensee's subsequent exploitation of the technology and is a common feature of most licences. The parties will have to agree what would be the appropriate royalty rate. The general rule of thumb is that the earlier the stage at which the technology was licensed out and the more development work that has been carried out and risk incurred by the licensee, the lower the royalty rate should be. A common problem is licensors not being paid all the royalties due to them, often due to a genuine oversight by the licensee, rather than because the licensee is deliberately trying to dodge payments. This risk is lessened if the licensor has the right to examine the licensee's records in order to verify that royalties are being correctly calculated. However, in such circumstances, the licensee will only want such audits to take place on reasonable notice and during business hours, and for anything to be revealed in the course of any such audit to be kept confidential. The licensee may also want audits to occur at a set regularity (for example, not more than once per annum) as frequent audits can be an administrative burden. The licensor, on the other hand, may want the licensee to pay the costs of any such audit if it reveals an underpayment in royalties.

- A final point worth making is that if the finished product comprises elements licensed in from a number of licensors who are all due a royalty, the licensee could end up paying royalties to so many parties that its own profit margin is eroded. In such circumstances the licensee may wish to include a royalty capping provision, to ensure that it never has to pay out more than a set percentage of its overall revenue to all its licensors in aggregate.

Since the payment provisions of a licence (or any other IP contract for that matter) obviously contemplate money changing hands, there will inevitably be tax ramifications. You should therefore seek advice from your accountants as to what would be the most tax-efficient structure for the transaction and balance this up against the other considerations. A structure which minimises the tax liability may go against what the parties wish to achieve in other respects. You don't want the tax tail wagging the deal dog, as it were.

The licensee may wish to grant sub-licences of its rights to third parties. In such circumstances, the licensor may only wish sub-licences to be granted with its prior written consent so that it can ensure that sub-licensees appointed have sufficient expertise and resources and/or are not competitors of the licensor. The licensor will also want to receive a royalty based on the revenue which the licensee receives from such sub-licensees as well as from its own sales.

The licensee could incur significant liability if it starts exploiting the intellectual property only to find that a third party is alleging that it is infringing that third party's IP in doing so. To guard against this, the licensee will therefore want to demand a warranty that the licensor can license the IP under the agreement without such third-party rights being infringed. If the technology in question is protected by patents then the licensor may just not know if exploiting it could infringe somebody else's patent rights somewhere in the world and may therefore wish this warranty to be qualified by 'so far as the licensor is aware'. Conversely, the licensor will want the licensee to indemnify it against any liability arising in connection with the supply of products or use of processes derived from the technology licensed.

If the licence is sole or exclusive, then the licensor will want the agreement to preclude the licensee from being involved in the development and/or commercialisation of competing products or processes. Moreover, the licence may be granted for a finite period or for the life of the intellectual property in question (e.g. for the unexpired 20-year term of any patent or for as long as any know-how licensed remains confidential). Either party may wish to terminate the licence if the other party is in material breach of any of its obligations or becomes insolvent. Such rights of termination are, in any case, common in any type of contract. If either party wishes the right to terminate without reason then the other party will want this only to take place on reasonable notice and may want some sort of payment as compensation for the time and expense which it will incur locating another licensor or licensee, as the case may be. How long the notice period should be will depend on how long it is likely to take the party on the receiving end of termination to wind down its operations and find another partner.

Finally, the licensor will want the licensee to inform it if the IP being licensed is being infringed or subject to an allegation that it infringes any third party's rights. Ideally, the licensee would want to oblige the licensor to diligently defend the IP against any such infringement or third-party allegations. As has been said, under English law an exclusive licensee of a patent has the right to do this as if it were a proprietor. The licensee should also seek to have this right expressly written into the contract. Similarly, the licensee ought to impose on the licensor an obligation to obtain as much registered IP protection as possible for the rights being licensed. The contract may include the right for the licensee to take over this responsibility should the licensor fail to meet it.

Liability and legality

If a party is in breach under a contract and the other party suffers loss as a result, it could make a substantial claim for damages. If the loss is serious enough, this claim for damages could be so high that it might even wipe out the company at fault. With this in mind, you should always ensure that you have adequate insurance. Companies may also wish to cap their liability under a contract so that, whatever the loss suffered, the other side cannot claim above a certain amount. However, under English law one cannot exclude all liability for death or personal injury caused by negligence and can only exclude or limit other liability to the extent that it is reasonable to do so. Other legal systems contain similar rules. This means that if a breach by you has the potential to cause the other side a high level of damage and yet your liability is capped at a ridiculously low level or excluded altogether, there is a danger of that limit on liability being challenged in the courts for being unreasonable and even set aside. As a result, legal advice should always be taken when deciding on liability.

You should also be wary of provisions in a contract which may be illegal or unenforceable for other reasons, particularly if you are contracting with overseas parties. The most important area of law for which this is the case is competition or anti-trust law. This subject really merits an entire book in itself and therefore will not be dealt with in any detail here. However, suffice it to say that intellectual property contracts often impose restrictions or confer exclusivity in a manner which could be in breach of national or European competition law principles. If this happens, you may be in danger of parts of the agreement (or even all of it) being unenforceable or being investigated (and possibly even fined) by the competition authorities. You should therefore always check with your legal advisers that your commercial arrangements will not get you into trouble in this regard. This is all the more important for large or dominant companies, because they have a significant market share and therefore anything they do is more likely to have a distorting effect on the relevant market which could lead to the unwelcome attention of the competition authorities.

Disputes, law and jurisdiction

As we point out in Chapter 5, everyone wishes to avoid litigation. As a result, any IP contract should provide in clear and effective terms that in the event of a dispute the parties will do their best to resolve it amicably. Where the agreement entails a long-term relationship, such as in a research collaboration or commercial licence, the parties could set up a coordination committee to monitor progress under the contract via regular meetings. This means that there is a much better chance that, in the event of a problem occurring, it will be addressed early on instead of being left to get worse until the parties fall out. If the personnel involved in the day-to-day running of the contract or such coordination committee cannot resolve the matter then it could be referred to the CEOs or other senior members of the company who, with a more global and objective view, might be able to succeed where others have failed.

If the parties cannot sort the dispute out between themselves, then there are alternatives to litigation. Firstly, mediation is becoming increasingly popular in this country. If they took this route, the parties would refer the matter to a mediator, for example one recommended by the Centre for Effective Dispute Resolution. The advantage of mediation is that it has a high success rate and is flexible and confidential. However, the mediator will not impose a decision on the parties, but rather will invite them to find a solution themselves. As a result, if no solution can be found the parties may still have to resort to the courts. Mediation may therefore not be suitable where the relationship between the parties is completely unsalvageable.

Arbitration is also confidential but can be expensive and protracted. It therefore tends to favour the party with the deepest pockets. Furthermore, if arbitration is to be contemplated then the parties should ensure that there is a clause in the contract specifying the arbitral system, the place of arbitration and the number of arbitrators. You should take advice from your lawyer when determining these.

Litigation, i.e. having the dispute resolved by the courts, can be time-consuming and expensive. Furthermore, since it is not confidential, it can result in bad publicity which can lead to a fall in share price. Of course, if litigation results in your company winning a swift and decisive victory then it can result in good publicity and, furthermore, deter other companies who might otherwise have intended to cause trouble.

If your contract is with an overseas party then there is scope, in the event of a dispute, for that party to argue that the courts of its country should hear the dispute. You will obviously wish to avoid this because of the increased expense and inconvenience of litigating abroad, using an unfamiliar legal system (which means instructing foreign lawyers) and possibly even a foreign language as well. Furthermore, the courts of many countries are biased against overseas litigants. You should therefore ideally insist that the contract provide for English law and the exclusive jurisdiction of the English courts to apply in the event of a dispute. Naturally, the other side may want the law and jurisdiction of its country to apply and as a result this is often one of the most negotiated points in a contract. Sometimes the solution is to choose the law and jurisdiction of a neutral country acceptable to both sides. Another compromise is for the law and jurisdiction of the injured party to apply. However, you should always take legal advice when deciding this issue.

Negotiating contracts

In negotiating IP agreements, as with any other contract, it is best to the designate primary negotiators. Of course, a large company may have a range of personnel to draw upon in this regard. Conversely, a smaller company may be less experienced and may involve fewer negotiators but as a result may be able to make decisions more quickly. Furthermore, you should give thought to whether you wish to negotiate the contract directly with the other side or via your respective legal representatives. At the early stages, when the broad terms are being thrashed out and the relationship is being built, it may be overly confrontational to involve the lawyers. However, they should certainly be involved at the later stages of negotiation. Less experienced companies may want to sound them out on key points at the earlier stages also, even if they remain in the background. Otherwise they may agree something early on, realise after input from their lawyers that it was inadvisable, and then have to make a U-turn which would disconcert or annoy the other side. The same principle applies in connection with the involvement of accountants and other professional advisers. In negotiating contracts, it is also helpful to agree a timetable for completion but don't be surprised if it overruns!

Finally, when negotiating with parties from other countries you should be aware of the business culture and negotiating style of those nationalities. For example, in Japan and the Middle East building up the relationship beforehand is very important and more will be accomplished by face-to-face meetings than by telephone or written correspondence. The same is the case in China (a rapidly expanding market for a range of sectors) in which it is also important to have a local contact who can put you in touch with the right people. In northern Europe business people are more keen on setting goals and deadlines whereas the approach is somewhat more relaxed in the south.

Of course, these are up to a point generalisations and it would be dangerous to apply them rigidly across the board. However, disregarding national factors can be equally dangerous.

4

Good intellectual property maintenance and management

In this chapter we will look at the protection of owned and (internally and externally) generated rights, at the various tools available to help to protect and maintain rights, and at the importance of seeking to avoid infringing the IP rights of others.

Protection of owned and generated rights

Any enterprise which owns, generates or uses intellectual property rights ought at all times to be aware of what those rights are, what new rights are being generated during the daily operation of the company and how to maintain and protect those rights at all times. Like land, stock and buildings, these rights are assets of the company and they need to be looked after.

The nature of the task here will differ according to and to some extent depending on the nature of the company.

- A company involved in the design and manufacture of shoes, perhaps through the use of both in-house and externally retained designers, will generate designs capable of protection under the European or United Kingdom design rights registration regimes. Such a company will need constantly to be aware of what rights are being created, and have a system in place to ensure that it decides whether an application for protection is appropriate in any particular case and if so that it is made in a timely way.

- A software company employing in-house programmers will similarly be creating copyright works (which may be potentially patentable in some jurisdictions) during the day-to-day operation of the business, and will need to ensure systems are in place to protect these rights and potential rights.

- Any company trading will do so under a business name, which will probably but not necessarily be its company name, and perhaps associated branding or logos. Its products are likely to have brand names. These company and product names are trade marks, and it is appropriate to consider whether they should be registered and, if so, in what territories (UK and foreign) a registration should be sought.

- Nearly all companies operate websites. These days domain names are just as important in many ways as trade marks and perform a similar function. They operate as the address of the business premises of the company on the Internet, and just like any address it needs to tell its customers and potential customers where it is and how to get to it. It is always necessary to consider whether the company's business name (and perhaps even product names) should be registered as domain names and what 'protective' registrations should be in place either for the purpose of deterring cybersquatters or rivals from registering or to pave the way for potential entry into a new product or geographical area (see further Chapter 2).

Thus is can be seen that the nature of the task will depend on the nature of the problem. What are some common themes in ensuring rights are protected?

Patent and trade mark attorneys

We have emphasised throughout this book the benefits of the effective use of patent and trade mark attorneys. Along with solicitors and where necessary barristers, these are key professionals. It is vital to use the right person for the right job at the right time. Patent and trade mark attorneys usually form the 'front line' in the protection armoury. Subject of course to the nature of the business and cost considerations, it is usually beneficial to involve them in all IP aspects of the business.

When selecting a product or company name, consultation with one's trade mark attorney is of immense benefit. They will be aware generally through professional knowledge and their access to complex searching systems whether a desired name is likely to be registrable and can steer one towards suitable candidates. As mentioned in Chapter 2, the more descriptive of products or services the less registrable is a trade mark. It is always a good idea when considering new product or company names to get the views of your trade mark attorney. They often have good ideas themselves and can certainly steer you in the right direction. Even if you are charged for this sort of feedback it is usually money well spent. Many hours have been wasted on working up branding later to be abandoned when a timely word with your trade mark attorney could have set you in the right direction in the first place.

With registration of patents and designs, patent attorneys, who will usually be experienced in the particular area of technology, play a crucial part in steering an applicant towards patentable matter or a registrable design.

At the early stages of dispute resolution or licensing discussions patent and trade mark attorneys, sometimes in consultation with solicitors, can provide cost-effective early assistance. It is also important in this context that everyone understands their own role and its limitations. A good patent/trade mark attorney will know when to bring in solicitor assistance or suggest that a solicitor take over conduct of the potential dispute or discussions. The two should where appropriate work together to provide a seamless and cost-effective service. Normally your patent or trade mark attorney will be your first port of call.

Ownership of internally generated intellectual property

As can be seen from the examples listed above, during the course of their work for the company employees and directors will often generate intellectual property rights, in many cases without anyone realising this is being done. These are primarily copyright protected works, patentable subject matter and designs.

The relevant legislation contains provisions which vary to some extent across the range of intellectual property rights but which usually vest intellectual property rights in the employer if they are generated during the course of employment. Nevertheless it is highly recommended to have the appropriate provisions vesting relevant intellectual property in employers in all employment contracts.

In the case of directors, there may not be any contract with the company and they may not be employees. If the intention is that rights generated by directors are to be owned by the company it is necessary to ensure the appropriate assignments are in place. These are not complex documents, but advice should always be sought in any specific case. In the case of patents directors are often wrongly named as 'inventors'. The position concerning inventorship should be properly recorded and proper arrangements made to vest ownership in the right legal entity. Not doing so can lead to expensive disputes. It is also worth noting that in the USA naming as inventors on the patent application individuals who did not genuinely perform that role can undermine the application.

Ownership of externally generated intellectual property

Many intellectual property rights are generated outside the company, by retained professionals, designers, consultants and the like. This often leads to a situation where, although paid for their work, the outside consultant might retain some rights in the intellectual property generated during the commission of the job.

This is often overlooked as people take the understandable but fundamentally wrong view that once they have paid for a job they are the owners of all rights in the work product. They might own the product itself, but the intellectual property in it is a separate legal right. Who owns the rights is subject to a separate legal decision and the position varies depending on which rights are involved (see further Chapter 2). The courts will often imply a term in contracts which provides that ownership of the intellectual property rights will vest in the commissioning company. However, this is always subject to what is often an exhaustive and expensive analysis of what the parties agreed, and the creator's standard terms of trade may provide specifically that it is the owner of the intellectual property rights. In that event a court cannot and will not intervene. It is also the case that if the party being commissioned is asked at the time of the commission to assign the rights, it is more amenable because it wants to get the work. If it is asked to effect an assignment at a later time when the rights are seen to be more valuable, it may try to use the position to leverage further payments.

Examples

- A company employs a web designer to create its website. The web designer uses its standard terms of trade. These provide that it will be the owner of all intellectual property rights (effectively copyright) in the work product (the website) subject to a licence to the client to use the site for the normal purposes of its business. The designer is paid, time moves on and substantial changes are necessary to the source code in order for the site to describe and service a new area of business. Before the changes can be made the owner of the copyright will have to agree to them and even if not involved in the work to make the changes will be entitled to a reasonable fee for the changes to the copyright work. This could have been prevented by the client ensuring that the copyright in the site was assigned on payment of the web designer's fee. However, a web designer needs to be careful that it only assigns such rights as are necessary. If a web designer uses underlying code which it wants to re-use for other projects, this should only be licensed.

- A particularly well-known footwear brand commissions an outside designer to create a logo. The agreement with the designer provides that the copyright in the logo shall remain with the designer but that the client may use it in any way connected with its business of selling shoes. The company prospers and years pass. The company starts to use the logo on various new ranges of goods – belts, handbags and clothing. They make substantial profits from these new parts of the business. Subject to any implied provisions in the agreement the company will be obliged to cease such use on demand or more likely pay the designer a reasonable royalty on sales of goods other than shoes bearing the design.

Many would regard these sorts of scenario as unfair for the company. However, English law generally permits freedom to contract on any terms the parties wish. True, a court will usually try to seek a fair result where that is possible. Note, however, that in the last example it would not necessarily be unfair for the designer to take the position he did. Had he known it would become such a widely used logo he might have wanted a higher price for the work. Limiting the use of the logo is a way of building that in.

From a company point of view the lesson here is to read the contract. Be familiar with what terms are being offered and accepted by each side, and if you need to ensure that there is an assignment of an intellectual property right in a contract for work product, make sure that it is in the contract. Depending on budget, get legal input on this issue.

Intellectual Property

Keeping information confidential

We have described in Chapter 2 what we mean by the terms 'know-how' and 'confidential information'. Know-how generated by employees and company operations should where appropriate be kept confidential through the use of non-disclosure agreements. If a company is seeking to enter into discussions for a joint venture on a new product or development it might be appropriate to enter into a confidentiality or non-disclosure agreement (NDA). These are dealt with in more detail in Chapter 3.

It is also sensible to keep the information known to as few people as possible, and for all copies of any physical records of it (usually this will just include documents but it might apply for example to a video tape) to be returned to the provider at the end of the project or a specified time. It is also important that information which is claimed to be confidential is treated as confidential. Leaving confidential information in places where it can easily be seen by casual passers by may cause the information to lose its confidentiality.

Example

- An inventor has a brilliant idea for the development of a solar powered engine. He has not the resources to develop this himself and he knows that some of the technical aspects of the idea need specialist input from a substantial car company. He also knows that if he approaches the company even in circumstances of confidence he is likely, human nature being what it is, to lose the idea once he discloses it. The information (know-how) is highly valuable but the only way to protect it at the moment until a patent application is filed is by the law of confidential information. A properly drafted NDA will allow discussions to take place without the value of the information being lost.

Know-how and confidential information might also need to be kept secret in this scenario in order for it to be capable of enjoying intellectual property protection. As mentioned in Chapter 2, there are a number of intellectual property rights which depend on being 'new', and once disclosed other than on terms of confidence an invention/design is generally not protectable. There are exceptions to this rule and information can be used if properly protected by an NDA. However, this is a particularly complex and important area and advice should always be sought from a properly qualified patent attorney or solicitor.

Protecting against infringement of others' rights

One needs to be aware of and avoid infringing, so far as that is possible, the intellectual property rights of others. Infringement of intellectual property rights is usually an expensive mistake. Even relatively minor disputes can be legally complex and there are many cases where the costs of getting involved in a dispute can be substantial.

There is in some cases a limited defence to an allegation of infringement of intellectual property rights on the basis that the infringer is acting 'innocently'. However, this issue itself (infringement or not) often generates considerable and expensive litigation and it is always best so far as one can to adopt a proactive approach to seeking to avoid disputes. Of course once a dispute or potential dispute is in train, different and more specific strategies are needed (see below in Chapter 5).

How then does one go about avoiding infringing unknown intellectual property rights of others? This is of course a difficult task, and it is not always attainable. The rights may be registered (e.g. patents, registered designs, trade marks) or unregistered (e.g. confidential information, copyright, unregistered designs). They might be owned by domestic or foreign companies. Indeed they might be domestic or foreign-based rights, since for example the United Kingdom in effect recognises the copyright owned by the citizens and corporations of the US (and many other countries). Once someone's toes have been trodden on, that is not an end to the matter. There is then the issue of whether infringement has in fact occurred, which is a legal question.

There are broadly two ways of approaching the task of seeking to avoid misuse of the rights of others, and what is done in any given case will largely depend on the business itself. These are:

- timely and prudent use of trade mark and patent attorneys, and where appropriate of lawyers; and

- maintaining general awareness of and sensitivity to the rights owned by competitors, either existing or new entrants on the scene. We deal with this aspect in the next section below.

The use of trade mark and patent attorneys is just as important in avoiding infringement of the rights of others as it is for protecting your own.

One of the most often repeated mistakes we see day to day is the adoption of trade marks without input from an agent. As explained above, clearance checks for trade marks can be as simple or as complex as the budget allows, from merely checking the local register to what agents call a full availability search, which will include checking phone books, the Internet and other sources to see whether others are trading using the mark in question. The most important thing, however, is not so much the extent of the search, which is largely dictated by outside factors, but when it takes place. All too often we receive a call from a client who is about to launch a product and wonders whether it might be a good idea to ask a lawyer about the trade mark and whether its use is 'OK'. The brochures have been printed, the advertising contracts are in place, everything has been done except the most important! This reveals a number of errors, all simple and all avoidable. It is all about timing – get advice early.

Of course the same applies in relation to designs and patents. Be aware that there is a registry and that it is possible to search it. Always use an expert to do the search – they should do it properly. What is done in any given situation will of course largely depend on the budget and very often it is not possible to be certain before going to market, but at least do the analysis and if problems occur be ready to react (see below).

General awareness and training

This is important both for maintaining and protecting one's own rights, and avoiding infringing the rights of others.

It is largely about practical steps to ensure that if an intellectual property 'light' goes on, the issue is quickly fed through to the appropriate individual or individuals in the company who will as necessary liaise with outside consultants to see whether a problem exists. This applies both to ensuring rights are maintained and protected and avoiding or dealing with claims relating to the infringement of the rights of others.

What is necessary and appropriate will vary from company to company. A substantial plc manufacturer with a large patent portfolio or a famous brand with a large trade mark portfolio will already be aware of the need to maintain and properly organise it and be familiar with the various systems and procedures it can adopt.

Most smaller businesses themselves own a range of IP rights, and might come into conflict with a range of potential problems arising from the use of the rights of others. They might have a flagship product, sold under a particular trade mark with its design registered. Maintaining and protecting these rights is relatively simple, and largely done by patent/ trade mark attorneys. Typically a company will be aware in general terms of the brands and rights of its competitors, and in the case of new rivals one should be able to tell (with a little professional help) from the product itself or associated material whether rights are or are likely to be claimed and searches are necessary.

Of course IP rights are not generally industry specific, so it may be that the rights of a non-competing company in a different area of business are inadvertently infringed with no potential for commercial damage. In that event there might be other ways of resolving the problem than arguing the point. It might be appropriate in this case to take a licence (or to grant one if you are the right owner). Many potential disputes become opportunities for a mutual licensing deal.

Meta-tags and websites generally

Meta-tags deserve a special mention. At the time of writing, the issue of whether and to what extent the use in meta-tags of the business or trade name of a competitor will infringe a trade mark or amount to passing off is still somewhat uncertain. This practice involves taking and deliberately inserting in one's meta-text (the hidden text underlying a website) the trade or product names of others.

Until a relatively recent UK case it was assumed by most lawyers that this would be an illegitimate activity and invariably amount to passing off or trade mark infringement, but that case has thrown some doubt on the issue. It is prudent, however, to avoid any potential dispute by avoiding such activity, not least because the law on this point may be different in different jurisdictions. The same point applies to other visible material on websites, which are usually generated and maintained by a variety of outside and internal contributors. Ensure that all contributors use licensed or company-derived sources, do not insert the meta-tags of competitors in the hidden text (it happens all too often) and test for compliance. Check the site and ask where the material which is not recognised was derived from. Where appropriate obtain warranties and assignments from outside contributors.

Summary

Any company of any size has an HR manager who will attend seminars/work with outside advisers and keep, at least to some extent, up to date with developments. We rarely see this repeated with intellectual property law, and IP law changes nearly as much as employment law! We must stress that it is not necessary to be familiar with the intricacies of intellectual property law, just know when a potential problem exists and when and where to go to fix it. It is also worth repeating that before asserting IP rights it is always appropriate to bear in mind the threats provisions and get appropriate advice.

No matter how careful one is there is always the possibility that the rights of others will be inadvertently trespassed upon, or that others will trespass on the company's rights. This will require rapid assessment of the problem to find the best solution and may involve litigation or dispute resolution. We deal further with this in Chapter 5 below.

The principles behind good intellectual property maintenance and management are simple:

- be familiar with the rights the company is generating or owns;

- ensure that proper systems are in place for their registration, protection and enforcement;

- be sensitive to the rights of others;

- when problems do arise deal with them quickly and look for positive solutions to help avoid costly and time-consuming disputes.

5

Dealing with intellectual property disputes

Introduction

This section will look at managing intellectual property disputes, from the point of view of the parties. We will look at some of the basics of litigation and explore how it is best managed and – where possible – resolved. This is not intended to be a detailed analysis of the workings of the UK judicial system and it is always necessary to seek specific advice, but we hope that we can assist in giving some insight into the way in which things work.

Nature of litigation

Intellectual property litigation has a reputation for being expensive. It is usually legally complex. Of the remedies sought, the injunction (preventing the infringement in the future) is usually much more important than damages (compensation for infringement in the past). As pointed out above, it is surprising how few cases yield any substantial damages. It is far more important in most cases to put a stop to the offending behaviour so the company can go on doing what it does best.

Despite the many judicial and other warnings issued about the danger of litigating rather than resolving disputes, potential litigants often come to lawyers with high expectations that the legal system will deliver what is to them a just result. Perhaps the most important quality for a litigant is flexibility and knowing when to walk away. Our legal system in this area has changed radically over the last few years. It has even changed its name from 'litigation' (a lawyer-oriented term focusing on the process) to 'dispute resolution' (a party-based term focusing on the aim of the process). Lawyers and judges have come to recognise that substance and result are far more important than form and technical process. The system has got better. Far fewer cases now reach trial and more disputes are resolved in a cost-effective fashion. However, the system has remained in many ways just as complex and expensive. Care is needed when navigating a way through it.

The English system and interrelationship with other parts of Europe

English law is derived from statute and judge-made or 'common' law. In the intellectual property field, as in many others, a substantial proportion of our legal rules emanate from European sources, either English law which is based on Directives from the European Parliament or on legislation or regulation coming from Europe which has direct effect in the EU member countries.

Historically speaking, the English system has much more in common with the law of the old Commonwealth countries such as India, Australia and New Zealand than it does with the systems of its European partners, which rely more closely on a very detailed codified system of written laws.

With European integration, the EU systems are coming closer together, and taking on the characteristics of each other's systems recognised as working better than the home-grown equivalents. This is partly driven by the perceived need for integration but it is also partly an evolutionary process, by which we mean that characteristics of any particular system which do not meet the needs of the public they serve are discarded. Because the same rights are often registered in different EU countries it is often possible in intellectual property litigation to 'forum shop', meaning to make a decision to sue in one EU country or another with the result applying across the whole or parts of the EU. Germany has acquired a good reputation for deciding patent disputes in a quick and cost-effective manner, spurring on the UK, which had a traditional reputation of being a reliable (if expensive and time-consuming) place to litigate patent disputes, to evolve to become much quicker and more cost effective, simply in order to attract 'customers'.

The Civil Procedure Rules

We will now look at the effect of the Civil Procedure Rules ('CPR') and how they operate in individual cases. Most non-lawyers' understanding of the way the system operates is based on a combination of real knowledge, scraps of information and just half understood know-how of how the process operates. The object of the CPR, which were introduced in the late 1990s, was to revolutionise the system, to sweep away many of the old ways of doing things and make dispute resolution faster, better and cheaper. It was an ambitious aim and it has in large measure succeeded. Thus coming to law now is different. When you consult your lawyer on dispute resolution it is important to do so with an open mind and be prepared to adopt tactical means and methods that might seem anathema to an understanding of the law lawyers had built in the past.

Practical aims of the CPR

How do the rules seek to make dispute resolution faster, better and cheaper?

1. *By the introduction of pre-action protocols.* These are simply sets of rules parties and their lawyers are obliged to follow. There are some that apply to specific types of dispute resolution. For intellectual property cases, the 'standard' protocol applies. The protocol sets out suggested time limits for the provision of information to your opponent, listing what information ought to be provided. The protocol states that if both parties or either of them fail to comply with it, the court has power to award costs against the non-complying party. The idea is to encourage early disclosure of one's case and genuine attempts to settle, and to punish parties who fail to do so, or who have failed to enter into alternative dispute resolution with a view to securing settlement. A copy of the standard Protocol can be seen at *www.dca.gov.uk/civil/procrules_fin/*; click on 'Pre-Action Protocols'.

2. *By simplifying the disclosure process.* Traditionally, parties were obliged to disclose to each other all relevant documents, without restriction. Courts now regularly make limited orders, focusing on what is really helpful to resolving the case.

3. *By the introduction of costs orders* to take effect at different stages of the proceedings, and 'issue-based' costs orders, so that even if you win you might lose some of your costs if you took a point which failed. Costs are traditionally a significant and sometimes the most significant factor in a case. By these means parties are encouraged to think whether they really ought to be taking this stance if they lose on costs rather than throwing in makeweight arguments.

4. *By allowing for Part 36 offers.* The rules have provisions allowing a party to make an offer to settle before or after a claim has started. If the offer is refused and the party making it does 'better' at trial, they are usually rewarded in costs and/or interest on damages. The idea is to encourage settlement offers. Thus if I am confident on the facts known by both sides that I can recover £20,000, the rules encourage me to make an offer for, say, £18,000, in the knowledge that although I may not achieve my goal of £20,000 my offer is likely to encourage my opponent to think hard about the risk of refusing it because I have the protection of the offer. Although there was discretion before in the case of costs this change in the rules has given much more certainty, and Part 36 with its 'reward system' is one of the most often used parts of the CPR.

5. *By taking control.* This is a key change. In common with our EU neighbours, judges take a much more active role in case management, ensuring that cases do not roll along in a leisurely way clogging up the courts and increasing costs. The courts will issue their own directions and follow them up if not complied with.

6. *By being more expensive.* It now costs more to go to

court. The fees for issue of proceedings as well as the cost of using the court have increased substantially since the introduction of CPR.

7. *By encouraging mediation or other alternative dispute resolution processes.* Mediation is the process of using a court or party-appointed independent third party who will in effect chair a settlement meeting. The mediation begins by each side putting their case to the other in open forum, after which there is flexibility in how things proceed. The usual course is for the mediator to take the temperature of the dispute with each side before engaging in 'shuttle diplomacy', travelling between the two groups seeking to find common ground. It is a delicate art. The mediator must try to find the common ground without revealing his inevitable knowledge of the opponent's case. In the end it is the parties who settle, and all the mediator can do is look for opportunities to put in front of them. Litigation may be the only option at the end of the day. There has been an explosion in mediation of cases in recent years. Courts cannot order parties to settle their cases. However, they can achieve much the same effect by the imposition of costs penalties on those who fail to try. Of course not every case is capable of settlement, mediated or otherwise. Some cases just need to go to court to be resolved, but not many. It is open to the parties themselves to try and settle their dispute. By the rules operating as they do this encourages parties to engage in informal dispute resolution of their own, either though correspondence including Part 36 offers or by meeting.

Some of these points are dealt with in more detail below.

Pre-action correspondence

The first step in any case is what is officially known as 'the letter of claim' but which most lawyers still call 'the letter before action'. This is a letter setting out the claim. This step is now governed by pre-action protocols.

As mentioned above, the aim of the pre-action protocols is to seek to avoid litigation. One of the most important ways of doing this is by encouraging the early disclosure of each party's case to the other, along with the major documents on which that party intends to rely. The protocols serve as a 'road map', focusing the parties on the issues and on the merits of each other's case. The courts will punish failure to comply with a protocol by appropriate costs orders. One has to be careful these days not to get caught up in massive pre-litigation correspondence generated as a result of a reluctance to be accused of having left no stone unturned before proceedings are commenced.

Nearly all intellectual property and other disputes are resolved by pre-action correspondence. Some larger cases will inevitably be the subject of court action. However, most of the time it is recognised that court action is just not economic for either party. This was the case before the CPR, though its introduction has improved things as it has focused on the need to set out the case more fully at the beginning.

From a party's point of view it is not usually necessary when defending or pursuing a minor infringement to spend vast amounts of time providing detail on the case to his lawyer. The lawyer ought to know what questions to ask in what areas, but it goes without saying it is important to be frank and complete in the information provided. Some disputes do go further and a failure to do this could be problematic down the road.

The typical letter before action will demand the following:

- an undertaking to cease the conduct complained of;
- delivery up of information which might assist in identifying other infringers;
- payment of costs and damages;
- delivery up or destruction of 'infringing goods', for example stock bearing the infringement mark or made according to the infringing process.

Although each case is different, many have very similar elements. In some cases there are a number of potential defendants identified over time nearly always carrying out the same activity, e.g. infringing a particular registered trade mark. It ought therefore to be possible in most cases to operate in a streamlined (and cost-effective) way.

Care needs to be taken with the threats provisions. These are dealt with in Chapter 2 and – it will be recalled – apply in different ways to different intellectual property rights. Because the threats provisions can cause problems down the line and because they can be avoided without compromising the strength of the assertion of rights it is always best to seek advice from a lawyer before asserting intellectual property rights. This does not mean a vast expenditure of money. If infringement is a frequent occurrence your lawyer ought to be able to provide standard documentation which he or you can use with minimal further lawyer input for individual cases.

At this stage a judicious combination of carrot and stick in the form of a Part 36 offer sent at the same time as a (properly worded) letter before action is often appropriate. As observed above Part 36 is perhaps the most significant weapon in the lawyer's armoury and should be used at any appropriate opportunity.

Just how any particular case is resolved will depend on a number of factors, such as the size of each party, the strength of the case and the available defences, and whether there is any common ground or opportunity to work together (surprisingly common). Once agreement is reached there will, if matters are properly attended to, be a legally enforceable contract, under which the potential claimant agrees to waive its claim as proposed in return for the defendant agreeing to comply with some or all of the demands identified above. Although the precise way in which a matter is resolved might sound like a technicality it is vitally important:

- from the point of view of the defendant, that the claimant has dropped the claim. A change of heart will do him no good. In addition the defendant can honestly declare that there are no outstanding claims against the company if this is needed for some purpose, e.g. a due diligence exercise;

- from the point of view of the claimant, that there will be an enforceable contract not to commit the wrong again. Thus in the event that such does occur all the claimant needs to do is to prove the contract, *not the intellectual property right*. So, for example, if a defendant promised in return for a waiver of claims not to import, deal in or sell an item of a particular type in which the claimant asserted copyright it would not be necessary were this to happen again to prove anything other than that it had happened, and this puts you in a much stronger bargaining position next time.

Two key points: from a defendant's point of view always

ensure that no admissions are made; from a claimant's point of view it is usually best to get the widest form of undertaking possible (although advice should always be taken so the undertaking is lawful and would not be regarded as anti-competitive). These points will always be a matter of bargaining.

The courts

Most UK intellectual property litigation is conducted in the High Court. The specialist Patents Court deals with patent and many other intellectual property litigation cases. In addition, the Patents County Court established about 15 years ago to deal with patents and design disputes is now becoming more widely used and its jurisdiction was recently extended to include trade mark cases.

It has been recognised that all forms of intellectual property litigation, and patent disputes in particular, are time-consuming, expensive and onerous. The Patents County Court is designed to deal with smaller, simpler cases as a cheaper alternative to the High Court. It has a good reputation and is often now used by substantial companies, although it was intended for use where parties could not afford the more expensive High Court. It now operates in competition with the High Court.

The court's case management powers

As mentioned above, another way in which the system changed substantially to encourage effective dispute resolution was the introduction of new powers for the court to manage its own cases. Traditionally, the system had, in contrast to those adopted in other European countries, largely provided a forum for parties to battle out a claim. The court did not see itself as having a positive role to play in dispute resolution; rather it was considered that the court's role was to adjudicate the contest, and provide rules under which the contest can be fairly conducted. Thus English courts have acquired a good reputation for fairness, but also have come to be regarded as expensive to use, rule-based and time-consuming.

This has changed. Under the new rules, for example, there is much more flexibility in the disclosure of documents; in particular, the courts now can and do order that discovery is restricted to particular issues or an issue. The courts now are much more selective and proactive in deciding what areas of evidence witnesses can give evidence on, whether there will be experiments, what discovery is to take place, and when the trial is to take place. In addition, costs awarded during the course of a case but before it goes to trial always used to be paid at the end of a case save in exceptional circumstances. Under the new rules, costs awarded at any particular point in the action must normally be paid then. This tends to focus the attention of parties and their advisers!

Offers to settle

We deal above with Part 36 of the Rules, which provides a formula for making settlement offers. In addition, it is open to a party at any stage of a dispute to make an offer to compromise it and to make that offer a 'without prejudice' one. If an offer has this status, it is 'privileged' and the judge is not made aware of it. The purpose of this rule is to encourage parties to enter into free discussions, and perhaps indicate they would make concessions to settle which they would not like the court to know of since it might be thought to indicate uncertainty about their position.

Not only will the offer itself but the surrounding circumstances including other things said or written in the context of the offer will be privileged. The thinking behind the rule is that it will encourage settlement by encouraging parties to be more open about the strengths and weaknesses of their case. Only genuine attempts to settle can attract the without prejudice rule. It is no good putting the words 'without prejudice' on a letter if all that letter does is to assert rights. There is great misunderstanding generally about the effect of these words and of their cooperation with the words 'subject to contract' (see below). However, broadly speaking:

- in order to attract the privilege, one should deem the conversation or letter to be 'without prejudice';
- it is not possible to obtain a benefit of the rule without there being genuine settlement discussions;
- during the course of without prejudice discussions, a *binding* agreement can be reached, and indeed that is the whole purpose of them.

In this last respect, the words 'without prejudice' do not mean the same as 'subject to contract'. What this latter formulation means is that any agreement is subject to a further contractual document, and the words 'subject to approval by a named party' or 'subject to ...' some other condition could just as easily have been inserted.

A variant on the without prejudice rule is discussions which are 'without prejudice save as to costs'. This means that anything said or written during the negotiations cannot be referred to openly, save in relation to costs. The purpose of this variation is to encourage negotiation. The idea is that an offer can be made in this context which will not be referred to the judge except when the question of costs comes to be decided. In that event it can be relied on to assert that the court should exercise its discretion on costs in your favour, for example if a reasonable offer was made and refused. So this rule operates in the same way as Part 36 offers, the latter providing a more formal framework.

Of course, in relation to any offer which seeks to take advantage of these principles, the offer needs to be pitched at the right level; you are taking a risk if you offer to settle for a little more than you can live with and then find that the offer is refused and you do not 'better' the offer at trial. That, of course, is another way the rules encourage settlement.

Although it is helpful to have a general understanding of how these terms operate, the way the rules operate in particular cases will depend on the precise application of complex rules, and advice should always be sought in individual cases.

Alternative dispute resolution

It is always open to either party to seek to resolve a claim, be it a contractual or right-based claim, by means of alternative dispute resolution (ADR). 'Alternative' simply means 'alternative to the court' and can include arbitration, mediation, informal negotiation, submission to some third party on a specific point or simply sitting around a table trying to settle a case. One or more of these ways of resolving disputes are often built into individual contracts (see above Chapter 3). We look below at these methods from the other point of view, when a dispute has broken out.

Arbitration

Many contracts provide for the appointment of an arbitrator in the event of a dispute. Most contract lawyers seek to avoid inserting clauses relating to arbitration because this form of ADR has become just as rule-based, time-consuming and expensive as the court system itself. While arbitration remains popular for some forms of dispute, e.g. building disputes, it is not substantially used in intellectual property cases.

Mediation

The process has already been described above. It is much more popular and less rule-based than arbitration and is often ordered by courts or selected by parties.

Other forms of dispute resolution

Most alternative dispute resolution is conducted by lawyers using 'without prejudice' or 'without prejudice save as to costs' correspondence, or even 'open correspondence', in seeking to persuade the other party through his lawyer of the strengths of their case. Although a mediation may be successful, it is expensive. It will usually involve at least a full day and the mediator as well as the lawyers and other parties present. Often, cases can be resolved by lawyers giving robust and sensible advice and cooperating with each other in seeking the resolution of a dispute. Key to the lawyer's task is to avoid costs escalating to such an extent that they become the issue rather than the amounts at stake in the dispute.

At the beginning of 2005, the Patents Act 1977 was

amended to provide a mechanism whereby any party could seek the opinion of an officer of the Patents Office as to the validity of or infringement of a patent. The opinion will be recorded on the Register (which means it will be open for viewing by any interested party) but it is not binding on the court or on the parties. The idea behind this move was to encourage another form of alternative dispute resolution, seeking the view of the Patent Office. Unfortunately, while the idea might be a good one, it is likely only to be used by a small number of defendants. It is cheap, but that is the very reason why a larger defendant or claimant would probably seek to avoid it as it would disentitle him to an advantage over his opponent. Of course, if the protagonists are roughly the same size and on the smaller side, they are more likely to use this system.

There are many other forms of alternative dispute resolution. There is no limit to how it can be conducted, provided that at the end there is a binding agreement which is clear and which sets out each party's rights in relation to the other. One particularly useful method is often to identify the real point of issue and then seek the opinion of a senior barrister such as a QC whose judgment is respected by both parties. In the case of intellectual property law, many experienced QCs sit as judges in the High Court, and if the point can be isolated and put before the QC, this might be a much cheaper way of resolving the dispute than going through the lengthy, cumbersome and expensive court procedures.

Insurance

In recent years there have been substantial changes in how litigation is funded. There are now many insurers, some specialising in IP, which provide a range of policies covering costs (yours and/or your opponents') and damages which might be payable. In addition, 'after the event' insurance is offered by many insurers. While it is popular for personal injury claims this is still a developing area in commercial cases, and whether it is appropriate for any particular case should be discussed with your solicitor. Also remember to check any existing policy to see whether the claim is covered.

Some checkpoints prior to litigation being initiated

Good intellectual property right management means ensuring that the rights remain healthy and ready for use. In a litigation context, many cases have been lost as a result of failure to check basic points, such as the party in whose name the right is registered.

For example, in a patent case, a subsidiary company may (for whatever reason) be registered as the owner of the patent, but litigation may be normally conducted by the parent company. In that case, it would be necessary to consider whether it was appropriate to assign the right to the parent company or for both parties to bring the claim. While it is a matter for lawyers to ensure that the right questions are asked, some of the key points are as follows:

- Is the right registered? Whose name is it registered under?
- Have the renewal fees been paid and are they up to date?
- Has any undertaking been given to anyone else in relation to the potential claim? Is there anything preventing the claimant from suing?

- If the right has been acquired, is the assignment valid? Has it been registered?

- Have the rights been dealt with in such a way as to impede the potential claim? For example, has the right to sue been waived or a licence given to the proposed defendant?

- Who is the best party to be the claimant? Who has actually suffered the loss? This may be a key point as no damages would be awarded if the party suing did not actually suffer any loss.

- Is the company insured? Is it appropriate to take out after the event insurance?

Remember, this is not an exhaustive list. Speak to your lawyer about preparing one for any given case.

Interim orders

At the same time as proceedings are started it may be appropriate to seek an interim order. This is an order that, pending the trial of the action, the alleged wrong be stopped, for example in a trade mark case the defendant is stopped from selling trade marked products. There are complex rules governing the operation of these orders but broadly speaking, if the claimant can establish that it will suffer unquantifiable damage (for example, by the abuse of its trade mark) and that it has a strong case, then it may be appropriate to apply for such an order.

In all cases it is necessary to move quickly as these orders are not normally granted if the claimant has allowed the wrong to continue so that the defendant would be prejudiced by it. For example, a claimant may assert that its trade mark is being infringed. If the defendant in the same field has started a new business selling the same type of article under a similar trade mark and is building it up it might be inappropriate to grant an interim order if the claimant does not promptly notify his rights, as the effect of being unable to trade until trial a year or so away might damage or destroy the defendant's fledgling business.

A court will not normally make such an order if damages are an adequate remedy. It has to be shown that the damage is unquantifiable, by which is meant not measurable in money. For example, severe and unquantifiable damage might be done to a famous sports goods trade mark if it were used by a small disreputable dealer in poor quality sports goods. It is hard, however, to characterise as unquantifiable the use by a substantial drug company of a process for manufacture of a drug alleged to infringe a patent owned by a (just as substantial) rival.

Normally these orders are granted on condition the claimant can ensure that the damages which might accrue to the other party are 'secured', i.e. money set aside to pay them, should he lose the case (in which case the order was not, in the result, justified).

Security for costs

Early in a case, a court will often be called on to consider whether any party bringing a claim or counterclaim ought to give 'security for costs'. This means providing security in funds or collateral for the other party's costs, or at least part of them, in the event that the claim fails. The idea is to provide some protection for the defendant for his costs if the claimant's case turns out to be unmeritorious and the defendant is in a poor financial position and cannot pay the costs of the winner. In the event of any counterclaim, an order for security for costs can sometimes be made against the defendant making that counterclaim, although this will depend on the circumstances. If the counterclaim is truly part of the way in which the defendant is defending the claim security will not normally be given.

Documents: privilege and disclosure

While most communications which would normally be regarded as confidential (e.g. doctor/patient, accountant/client) are not protected from disclosure to the other side in litigation, communications between a client and his legal adviser are generally regarded as protected from disclosure to the other side. If a solicitor writes a letter to his client outlining the strengths and weaknesses of his case, it would be regarded as unfair in the context of the dispute to which the letter related for the other party to be able to see that letter. Whether a particular document falls within the protected field is a legal question.

Documents often decide cases. Parties to prospective disputes (and their lawyers) are obliged to preserve documents that might be relevant to the case, although this can be disruptive to a business. It is always important to ensure that documents that do or might relate to a claim are retained and provided to your solicitors.

Document retention generates its own particular problems. The advent of e-mails is particularly problematic. Many e-mails are lost, misfiled or only part of them kept although the idea behind e-mails is to avoid paper. In fact, the result has been the opposite, because in any properly ordered system, hard copies should be kept of e-mails relevant to any transaction or case. That is often easier said than done.

As mentioned above, the rules on disclosure of documents require each party to disclose to the other documents which are relevant to the case. The courts now have wide powers to make restricted disclosure orders or orders for disclosure of certain classes of documents.

It is open to a party to apply for what is called 'pre-action disclosure' of documents if it can satisfy the court that it is necessary to see such documents in order to establish whether a claim can be made. In addition it is also open to parties to seek disclosure from third parties of documents which they believe such a third party has and which are relevant to the action.

A final word

It has been said that a man who litigates is either a fool or a millionaire and there is some justification in this claim. But sometimes it is necessary. The key is flexibility – remember that the aim of the process is not to seek justice, but to get as good a result as practicable and preserve and maintain your company and its assets. This usually means ending the case on terms you might not regard as perfect but which you can live with. It is vital to keep a constant eye on your costs. Ask your lawyer to provide a weekly costs report – at no charge!

6

Issues arising on change of ownership

Sale of business or change of control?

Intellectual property rights are assets and if another party is potentially interested in investing in or buying your business or company, then it will want to check out the value and integrity of the intellectual property just as much as it will the premises, plant and machinery, fixtures and fittings and so forth. In such circumstances, there are two ways in which another party may take over your business.

First, you might sell the business. In this scenario, company A sells the business to company B, 'the business' comprising the agreed list of assets, contracts, liabilities and so forth. Ownership of the assets of the business, including the intellectual property, will need transferring from company A to company B, according to the requirements outlined in Chapter 4 above.

On the other hand, company A may undergo a change of control. In such circumstances, company A remains the owner of the business and all of the assets in it, and it likewise remains the contracting party for the contracts which the business has entered into. However, whether due to a new round of investment, flotation on the stock exchange or acquisition by or merger with another company, its controlling shareholding has changed.

Questions that will be asked

The two alternatives outlined above are fundamentally different in nature. However, they both have a similar result, namely that a new party or collection of parties will be in control of the business. That party or collection of parties (which for the sake of simplicity we will call 'the buyer') will want to go through all aspects of the company with a fine-tooth comb before taking it over. This will obviously include all intellectual property aspects. In particular, the buyer will want answers to the following questions:

- What registered intellectual property rights does the company own? Have these been validly applied for? Have all application fees and renewal fees been paid on time and all other application requirements been met? For example, the company may have applied for a patent without obtaining an assignment of the rights in the relevant invention from the original inventors.

- Has the company obtained registered IP rights in the key territories in which it is manufacturing or selling? Conversely, is the company wasting money by maintaining IP rights which it doesn't exploit or in territories in which it doesn't operate? A detailed audit of many companies will reveal a surprising amount of rights falling into this category.

- Is the company currently applying for any registered IP rights? If so, what is the prospect of the application being granted? Have any objections been lodged by third parties during the application process?

- Has the company's IP ever infringed a third party's IPR or is there any possibility that such infringement is taking place at the moment? Similarly, has the company's IPR ever been infringed or is it currently being infringed by a third party? If the answer to any of these questions is 'yes', what measures have been taken? No buyer will want to inherit expensive patent or trade mark litigation.

- To what extent does the company's IPR constitute know-how? How is this documented? On a day-to-day basis, is that know-how kept confidential? To what extent does it reside in the heads of key employees whom the company will not want to lose? Will the company's impending sale make them want to leave? If they leave, are they adequately tied in by non-solicitation and non-competition obligations in their employment contracts?

- If the company has licensed any of its IP out are the licensees complying with the terms of the licences?

- If the company is using any third parties' IPR, is it complying with the terms of the licences entered into?

IP contract issues

Regarding IP contracts in general entered into by the company (which will fall into the categories detailed in Chapter 3 above):

- Are they reasonable or do they prejudice the company unduly, for example by imposing obligations which are difficult to attain, exposing the company to unacceptable liability or not giving the company accurate remuneration for what it is doing under the contract?

- Is the company in breach of any of its obligations under any such contracts? Is the other side? If the answer to either of these questions is 'yes', what measures have been taken as a result?

- Do any of the contracts contain clauses allowing the other side to terminate if the company either sells the business or undergoes a change of control? If so, the buyer could find that it loses the benefit of key contracts when it takes over the business. This could happen if the other party to any such contract is worried because it does not think that the buyer will be able to assume performance of the company's contractual obligations or because the buyer is a competitor of that other party. Ultimately, if any business is being sold or any company is going through a change of control, one of the first things which the buyer's lawyers will look for is contracts with such termination clauses in them. For this reason, you should if at all possible avoid entering into contracts which give the other side the right to terminate under such circumstances. If you enter into contracts containing such clauses, they could be a deterrent to any potential buyer.

- Are the contracts legal? Do they contain any clauses which might be unenforceable or contravene any applicable law or regulation? For example, the company may have entered into a licence or collaboration agreement which breaches national or European competition law. You should always take legal advice to minimise the risk of this happening because such contracts will, likewise, deter the buyers.

Due diligence and warranties

Obviously, the buyer will want to find out as much as it can about the company in order to obtain answers to these questions. It will do this by trawling through the company's records and documents, and asking questions of relevant employees. This process is called 'due diligence' and it can be a time-consuming, protracted and stressful exercise for both sides! It also requires the involvement of professional advisers who, of course, have to be paid. However, there are some things which the buyer will not be able to find out by due diligence and in such circumstances it will just have to take the company's word for it. To protect it in this regard, the contract governing the sale of the business or investment in the company will contain warranties, i.e. undertakings, that certain representations by the company are correct. If these representations are subsequently found to be untrue then this will constitute a breach of contract and the company or its sellers will have to pay damages.

In the context of IPR, such warranties might include the following:

> All fees for the application for and maintenance of registered intellectual property in respect of the company's IPR are up to date.

It may well be that this warranty is not absolutely correct, for example because the company is behind on some trade mark renewal fees. If this is the case, then the company must make an express written disclosure of the fact. If it does so, and the buyer completes the transaction in full knowledge of that disclosure, then the company will not be liable. However, if the company keeps its mouth shut and this problem comes to light after that transaction has been completed, then it could find a claim for breach of warranty coming its way. For this reason, it is always best to be honest and up front with the buyer, even if it makes the company a less attractive proposition in the short term. Sweeping problems under the carpet only causes worse problems later on and makes the company seem untrustworthy.

Another IPR warranty which the company might be obliged to give is:

> The company's IPR has never infringed or been infringed by the IPR of any third party.

This warranty is potentially dangerous because the company may, for example, just not know if someone is infringing its IPR somewhere in the world or if someone else somewhere in the world has a patent which the company's IPR is infringing. In such circumstances, therefore, the company will want to qualify this warranty with 'so far as it is aware' or 'to the best of its knowledge'. On the other hand the buyer may not stomach this. It may feel that it is acquiring a business or company in good faith and therefore should not have to bear the risk of potential liabilities which it can know nothing about. In such circumstances, who gets their own way depends on who has the most leverage in negotiations or on one party backing down for commercial reasons.

How to make the process easier

As can be seen from the above summary, selling a business or undergoing a change of control is a complicated business with numerous pitfalls. If you ever undergo the process,

Issues arising on change of ownership

you can make it much easier by adopting the following practices on a day-to-day basis from the business's inception:

- Keep well organised, detailed and up-to-date records of all intellectual property owned by, licensed in and licensed out by the company, and of any disputes, litigation or potential litigation connected with it.

- Liaise regularly with your lawyers and patent and trade mark attorney in order to ensure that all registered IP has been properly applied for and maintained.

- If you have taken over any IP from a third party, then make sure that the assignments are properly in place so that ownership of that IPR has incontrovertibly passed to you.

- Keep an up-to-date record of all contracts entered into by the company, catalogued according to the types detailed in Chapter 4 of this book. You should also keep copies of those contracts filed away for easy access, similarly categorised.

- Keep all contracts under regular review to ensure that both you and the other side are meeting your respective obligations under them. That way, any problems that arise under a contract which might otherwise escalate or which may require that contract to be revised can be dealt with early on.

- Always take legal advice to ensure that you are not about to sign or have not entered into a contract which is potentially illegal or unenforceable.

- Don't be so desperate to secure the deal that you enter into a contract which is, in commercial or legal terms, suicidal!

Intellectual Property

Companies which follow these rules generally find themselves in good order. This will make them more attractive to potential buyers and make the transaction less painless. Companies which don't follow these rules may find themselves:

- unable to locate a buyer – if they need a buyer to survive during tough times, they may then go under; or
- giving the buyer reasons to drive the price down.

In order to ensure the transaction goes ahead, deal with problems at the time rather than trying to patch them up after the event. For instance, if you own a patent but realise that your ownership is undermined by the fact that you never obtained an assignment of the invention from the original inventors, it may be difficult to subsequently remedy that problem if, for example, those inventors have gone their own way and cannot be located or if you have fallen out with them and they do not wish to cooperate. Alternatively, they may only cooperate if paid a hefty sum, which is obviously undesirable.

As was said at the beginning of this chapter, all of these issues don't just apply in the context of IPR, but in the context of all of the company's other assets, liabilities and contracts. This can make selling the business or undergoing a change of control a gruelling process, particularly for large or complicated companies.

7

How does IP affect your business in practice?

Introduction

This chapter contains a number of case studies to illustrate how intellectual property issues affect various different types of businesses. The case studies concern three imaginary companies in three different sectors – bioscience, software and consumer products – which are all dependent on and affected by IP rights but in significantly different ways. The case studies contain illustrations of what to do and what not to do in the light of the issues covered in the rest of this book. The case studies are admittedly simplified for ease of understanding and any real-life company will probably encounter a much wider range of issues during its lifetime. However, the issues covered here are typical of those encountered by companies in the sectors in question. We would stress that the companies detailed below are entirely imaginary and that any similarity with any particular company is unintentional and incidental. We have also done our best to use company names which, to our knowledge, are not used by real businesses. If it transpires that they are then we apologise and no connection should be inferred!

Bioscience

Three researchers from the Department of Medicine at Oxbridge University have been developing various chemical compounds which they think may have therapeutic qualities, particularly in the context of influenza-type diseases. Given the continuing international concern about the possibility of a flu pandemic they decide to set up a company to develop the technology further.

The researchers talk to the university's patent attorney who advises them that the compounds which they have come up with are possibly patentable and patent applications are therefore lodged in the UK with a view to lodging further applications in key territories in the rest of the world during the one-year priority period.

The researcher's employment contracts provide that all IP generated by them is owned by Oxbridge University. They therefore speak to the technology transfer officer at the university and come to an agreement that the IP can be spun out into a start-up company founded by the researchers subject to:

- the university being a shareholder in the company; and
- the company obtaining enough investment from other sources to make further commercialisation and development of technology viable.

The researchers therefore set up the company Oxbridge-flu Limited. However, pending finding laboratory premises of their own, they continue to use the university's laboratories and facilities. Meanwhile, they have put together a business plan with the help of the university technology transfer officer and various local entrepreneurs whom they have been introduced to.

The business plan succeeds in attracting an investor who

invests £1 million in the company. The university becomes a minority shareholder in Oxbridge-flu and in return transfers all its rights in the technology to Oxbridge-flu.

Since the company is at such an early stage and its technology so embryonic, the due diligence process is fairly simple. However, the investor does, during the due diligence process, discover two potentially serious hiccups, namely:

- One of the founders was part-funded during his research at Oxbridge University by a Japanese pharmaceutical company. The terms of the funding provide that the Japanese pharmaceutical company will be entitled to a 1 per cent royalty on all revenue from the commercialisation of technology developed as a result of that research. This will obviously eat into Oxbridge-flu's profit margin in the long term although as the company moves forward and widens its product portfolio, it will doubtless generate technology which falls outside the scope of this funding and which the Japanese company will therefore have no call on.

- As well as the three founders, one other academic was involved in creating the original invention. However, he wants to stay in academia and is not interested in commercialisation and therefore has not become involved in Oxbridge-flu. Nevertheless, for the company's ownership of the technology to be watertight, all his rights in the technology need assigning to Oxbridge-flu. The investor demands this as a prerequisite of signing the deal. Unfortunately, the founders of the company do not get on very well with this fourth inventor and therefore have to pay him a significant sum to hand his rights over. As a sweetener, they also make him a member of their scientific advisory board and give him a small shareholding in the company.

Intellectual Property

Now that Oxbridge-flu has obtained the £1 million of investment, it uses the money to:

- apply for further patents in key territories where it envisages its markets will be, namely Europe, the USA, Canada and Japan;

- hire a drug discovery company to screen its compounds against various disease targets. The agreement with the drug discovery company provides that all data generated from the screening will be kept confidential by the drug discovery company and owned by Oxbridge-flu; and

- lease laboratory premises. This means that the founders can move out of the university labs and cease being members of the university. They now concentrate on the company full time.

The screening data obtained from the drug discovery company leads Oxbridge-flu to believe that it could develop an effective vaccine to combat bird flu. It therefore carries out further research. It also contracts for further research to be carried out by its old contacts at Oxbridge University. The research agreement provides that the results of that research will be owned by Oxbridge-flu but the university will be granted a licence to use the results for internal research purposes only. The university will also be able to publish articles on the project findings subject to Oxbridge-flu first filing any necessary patent applications and the publications not containing any confidential information.

Eventually, Oxbridge-flu has a vaccine which it can test on humans in phase 1 clinical trials. Because it has reached this stage and filed further patents, it is successful in securing a further round of funding. Oxbridge-flu hires a contract manufacturer to formulate the vaccine and manufacture enough of it efficiently to be used in clinical trials. The contract manufacturer generates IP in the form of formulating and manufacturing processes. Under the contract, ownership of these processes is transferred to Oxbridge-flu so that Oxbridge-flu can subsequently use those processes itself or license other manufacturers to do so.

Phase 1 clinical trials are successful but Oxbridge-flu does not have the resources or expertise to conduct the larger-scale phase 2 and 3 clinical trials. At this point, therefore, it licenses the vaccine technology out to a large pharmaceutical company, Maxipill Inc. The terms of this licence are as follows:

- Maxipill will take over the responsibility for and cost of maintaining and defending the patent rights.
- Maxipill will be responsible for the phase 2 and 3 clinical trials.
- Maxipill will have an exclusive worldwide licence to exploit the vaccine.
- Maxipill will be responsible for obtaining market authorisations in all territories in which it will be selling the vaccine.

In return for the rights granted to Maxipill under the licence, Oxbridge-flu is paid:

- an upfront fee; and
- a milestone payment when Maxipill makes its first commercial sale in a key territory (i.e. in the European Union or America); and
- a royalty of 3 per cent on all net sales.

The vaccine gets through all subsequent regulatory hoops and is successfully marketed. Maxipill obtains trade mark protection for the name 'Banflu' in the territories which it is selling in and sells the vaccine under that brand.

After 18 months Maxipill discovers that the vaccine technology may possibly infringe the patent rights of one of its major competitors. Fortunately, Oxbridge-flu merely warranted in the licence that use of its technology did not infringe any third party's rights so far that it was aware. Maxipill investigates further and is advised by its patent attorneys that some of this other pharmaceutical company's technology arguably infringes some of Maxipill's patents. Rather than waste time suing each other, the companies enter into a mutually beneficial cross-licence agreement to tidy these issues up.

Software

Cadplane Limited is set up by three computer-aided design (CAD) software writers. They have left a large CAD software company because they want to go it alone. They are careful to ensure that the non-competition restriction in their employment contract has expired before they set up the new business and that they do not, going forward, use any code belonging to their previous employer. They commence the development of CAD software which can be used in aircraft design. Much of the code is written by subcontractors in India. In order to recoup funds after paying the subcontractors they succeed in obtaining funding from an outside investor. However, during the due diligence process, the investor discovers that they have not entered into any written contracts with these subcontractors. As a result, obligations are undefined and no performance criteria are imposed. Furthermore, the subcontractors are required to give no warranty that they have not infringed any third party's copyright in generating the code. Most crucially, in the absence of a written agreement providing for it, the

How does IP affect your business in practice?

subcontractors have not assigned their rights in the code to Cadplane.

As a prerequisite for providing funding, the investor therefore requires all subcontractors to enter into a written agreement with Cadplane addressing these issues. None of the subcontractors have a problem with this since they realise that if they do not cooperate they are unlikely to get any further work from Cadplane in the future. However, due to their location in India there are logistical problems and it takes a long time to get all the contracts signed.

Cadplane is now coming close to launching the product. It applies for patent protection in the US for the software but is advised that there is less chance of success in Europe, where software patents are harder to obtain. It therefore has to rely on copyright protection in Europe. It also hires a PR company to come up with a range of designs for Cadplane to use in a series of advertisements for the product in the aviation and IT press. Cadplane signs the PR company's standard terms of supply without reading them and the designs are produced. However, Cadplane feels that the designs can be improved on and, in any case, wishes to extend the run of advertisements. It therefore amends some of the designs supplied by the PR company and pays for a new run of advertisements incorporating the amended designs.

It gets an unpleasant surprise when the PR company sends it a letter before action, claiming copyright infringement. It claims that the designs were created for Cadplane for a specific range of adverts and Cadplane merely had an implied licence to use them for those adverts. However, in altering the designs, the letter continues, Cadplane is in breach because it signed up to the PR company's standard terms of supply which did not provide for copyright in the designs to be assigned to Cadplane. Cadplane is therefore infringing the PR company's copyright in the designs by reproducing

Intellectual Property

amended versions of them. Cadplane takes legal advice and is told that the PR company has a strong case. Cadplane therefore pays the PR company a significant sum of money in order to obtain the relevant rights.

Both these episodes convince Cadplane of the importance of signing written agreements and getting ownership of key IP and it decides to be much more careful in future. When it comes to licensing out the completed software package, Cadplane therefore has a proper form of licence agreement drawn up. The licence agreement which its customers are required to sign up to contains the following provisions:

- The licence is non-exclusive, since Cadplane sees the most advantage in licensing the package out to a range of companies in the aviation sector.

- The licence is restricted in the number of copies and users and is not assignable or sublicensable. This is so access to the software does not leak out into other companies which could be potential customers of Cadplane.

- There is an agreed installation and testing procedure to ensure that the software is fully compliant and accepted by the client before going live.

- Cadplane supplies fixes, patches and upgrades to the customer on a regular basis.

- The source code for the software is put in escrow so that it can be accessed by the clients if Cadplane ever becomes insolvent or is otherwise unable to continue to perform its licensing or support obligations.

Under a supplemental maintenance agreement, for an annual fee Cadplane supplies support to customers on an ongoing basis should anything go wrong with the software. This support comprises in the first instance advice over the telephone, followed by on-line assistance and an emergency call-out facility for more serious problems for which Cadplane charges extra. It only covers problems with Cadplane's product, not with the customer's other software or hardware, and it does not cover problems caused by the customer's unauthorised use or misuse of the product. Cadplane will charge its hourly rate if it chooses to fix these extra problems. In negotiations, some of Cadplane's customers succeed in including a service level in the agreement which Cadplane is contractually obliged to comply with. Consequently, in any year, if it falls short of meeting any agreed response times or fails to fix any problem within the requisite period, the following year's annual support fee will be reduced by a corresponding amount to compensate the customer.

Some of Cadplane's customers require the software to be tweaked or enhanced to address their particular needs. Cadplane is happy to do this for an extra fee. However, each customer which has requested such bespoke elements to the software wants to own the copyright in them also and preclude Cadplane from supplying them to its other customers. Cadplane is happy for its standard form licence agreement to be amended to reflect this, provided that it retains its ownership of and freedom to license out the original generic software and is free to create further bespoke elements for other customers who have similar needs.

Cadplane does very well and eventually attracts the attention of a large US CAD software company since Cadplane's increasing numbers of customers in America are making it a significant competitor of the US company. However, Cadplane's product is superior. In a lucrative acquisition, the US company therefore buys Cadplane and takes over its customers. However, the Cadplane founders don't like the idea of working for a large company again and therefore cut loose to set up a new company and develop a new product.

Consumer goods

Smiths Inc. have for many years sold various novelty toys in the United States and have long considered venturing into the UK market. They specialise in distinctive and unusual dolls. Most of these were designed by Vic Vulnerable, a US citizen and resident and CEO of Smiths, who sees it as a potentially lucrative market for their goods and as the natural entry point into the European market. Their products are all made in China and shipped to the various countries in which they sell. The prospective European launch is a significant step in the growth of the business. Smiths do not have any registered intellectual property rights in Europe.

Smiths decide to appoint a distributor, Maximus Ripoff, who Vic Vulnerable has met at a trade show. Maximus claims to know the UK doll market well and says he will be able to make lots of money for both Smiths as importer and Maximus as distributor. A 'home-made' distribution agreement prepared by Maximus is signed. It does not make any provision for goodwill from sales to vest in Smiths nor does it say anything about ownership of IP rights relating to the products. The termination provisions are vague – it is not clear what notice is needed or how long the agreement will last without renewal.

Smiths have decided to launch simultaneously in Australia, the US and Europe new products called BABA (a doll for girls) and BRIAN (a toy dog for boys). Each is a completely original distinctive design, created by Vic with input from external consultant designers in the US. Things go well for 12 months, until a letter before action is received from a firm of lawyers in Birmingham alleging that their client Toptoys Limited has for many years sold a toy dog under the name BRIAN, that they have a UK registered trade mark covering the name, and that the sale of toy dogs under that name amounts to passing off and trade mark infringement.

Negotiations ensue. These are initially left to Maximus who adopts an aggressive and combative approach. He refuses to enter into any discussions, claims the US reputation of the Smiths toys trumps any rights which Toptoys have and also refuses to provide any documents supporting his case in response to the requests from Toptoys. Being left with no option, Toptoys issues proceedings in the Patents County Court alleging trade mark infringement. Being caught up with developing his business in Australia, Vic leaves the progress of the case to Maximus and his lawyers. Things do not go well. Having had some experience of litigation in the UK some years ago, Vic had assumed that the case would take some time to get to trial and hoped that he could negotiate with Toptoys – and use his undoubted financial muscle – in the meantime. But he learns that the case is listed for trial shortly and that he stands little chance of success. Of substantial concern is the fact that Toptoys made a Part 36 offer before they sued which offered settlement on the basis that each party bore their own costs and that Smiths stopped using the name BRIAN in relation to its toys. The lawyers chosen by Maximus had not been keeping him up to date on costs, and Vic is horrified to learn that they have skyrocketed and that he is told he has little chance of success in the case, which is listed for the following week.

Vic did not get where he was by being tentative. His attention no longer diverted, he comes over to the UK, terminates Maximus' contract, and proposes talks with Toptoys. He learns very early on that Toptoys is a well-run family company with a good distribution network, but without the necessary manufacturing contacts to import high-quality merchandise into the UK for distribution throughout Europe. After two days of talks Vic has settled the dispute and appointed Toptoys as his EU distributor on terms prepared by Vic's new lawyers. But this comes at a cost. Maximus is seeking to take advantage of the vague terms of his distribution agreement to get a pay off and this has to be resolved. In addition Vic has to bear the costs of the action and of acquiring the trade mark BRIAN. The cost is to some extent offset because Toptoys are also very keen to do the deal, but all in all it has been an expensive exercise.

During the negotiations Toptoys' lawyers ask about IP protection for BABA and BRIAN. Vic cites his US design rights, which he has been careful to register. However, it becomes clear that Vic has failed to seek any registered design protection in the UK or Europe. He has not even taken advice on the subject. As the products have been in the market for over two years it is now too late to apply for such protection, thus depriving Smiths of a valuable and cost-effective means of protecting against copiers of the designs in Europe. There is a possibility of copyright protection for the items, but there are various problems, including a failure to obtain an assignment from one of the external consultant designers. This lessens the value of the goods as licensed product and Vic is unable to secure as good a deal on them as he had hoped, although he does (at a cost) have the trade mark rights.

Vic returns to Australia to continue his discussions with potential distributors, resolving from now on to put on the top of his list the need to check the local IP position every time he proposes to launch a new product or enters a new geographical territory.

8

Conclusion

We hope that this book has given you a good introduction to the nature and importance of intellectual property rights. Identifying and exploiting the intellectual property rights which are of relevance to the products or services which you offer can only enhance the value of your business. Of course, if you encounter any specific intellectual property issues then, although the general principles outlined in this book will be helpful, you will also need specific legal advice from intellectual property lawyers such as ourselves.

Firstly, it is worth bearing in mind that, as important as intellectual property is, a thorough understanding of it is not the only thing which will guarantee your business success. You may have an invention which is patentable and you may have the money to apply for patent protection in all the territories you want. However, none of this will do you much good unless that invention results in a product or process which either fills a gap in the market, creates a new market or is significantly ahead of the competition. Even then, it will need hard work, clever marketing and an effective distribution network to get it before the customers. In the same way, an author who assiduously hunts down copyright infringers can take small comfort from this if nobody wants to read his book anyway!

Intellectual property awareness is not a substitute for any of these attributes. It is an additional attribute which you will need if your business is to thrive but, as this book seeks to demonstrate, it is a crucial one nonetheless.

Appendix
Useful websites

General

- *http://www.wipo.int*
  Information about the World Intellectual Property Organisation including information about international trade marks, designs and patents.

- *http://www.informationcommissioner.gov.uk*
  Information concerning the protection of personal data under the Data Protection Act 1998 and the Freedom of Information Act 2000.

- *http://www.ipr-helpdesk.org*
  Provides information and advice about Community intellectual property protection.

Chapter 2

Patents

- *http://www.patent.gov.uk/patent/index.htm*
  Information and advice on patents and the application

process in the UK including a searchable database of patent records, downloadable forms and brochures and a fee schedule.

- *http://www.european-patent-office.org*
  Information on the procedure for obtaining a European patent including a guide to the application process and a list of fees, costs and prices.

Designs

- *http://www.patent.gov.uk/design/index.htm*
  Information and advice on designs and the process for registering a design in the UK including a searchable database of design records, downloadable forms and brochures and a fee schedule.

- *http://oami.eu.int/en/design/default.htm*
  Information on the Community design right including frequently asked questions regarding the registration procedure and a facility to apply to register a Community design online.

Registered trade marks

- *http://www.patent.gov.uk/tm/index.htm*
  Information and advice on designs and the process for registering a trade mark in the UK including a search facility for the trade marks register, downloadable forms and brochures and a fee schedule.

- *http://oami.eu.int/en/mark/default.htm*
  Information on the Community trade mark including frequently asked questions regarding the registration

procedure and a facility to apply to register a Community trade mark online.

Domain names

- *http://www.nominet.org.uk*
  Provides information about the registration of .uk domain names, including a facility to search the 'WHOIS' database. Also includes information about Nominet's dispute resolution procedure.

- *http://www.icann.org*
  The Internet Corporation for Assigned Names and Numbers website providing information about the Domain Name System (DNS) and IP and domain names generally.

- *http://www.icann.org/udrp/udrp.htm*
  Provides information on ICANN's uniform domain name dispute resolution policy.

- *http://www.archive.org*
  This site is a digital library of archived Internet sites, texts, audio, moving images and software.

- *http://www.dnsstuff.com*
  Information about systems administration matters including tools and applications to check WHOIS data, check an e-mail address for problems and guides to many other Internet-related issues.

Chapter 3

Research agreements

- *http://www.innovation.gov.uk/lambertagreements/*
  Provides model agreements and guidance notes for collaborative research projects.

Disputes, law and jurisdiction

- *http://www.cedr.co.uk*
  The website of the Centre for Effective Dispute Resolution provides general information about mediation and other dispute resolution methods.

- *http://www.adrgroup.co.uk*
  The website for ADR Group who provide alternative dispute resolution (ADR) services. Contains a list of key contacts and general information about ADR.

Licences

- *http://www.cla.co.uk*
  The website for the Copyright Licensing Agency provides information about copyright licensing both online and in the form of downloadable brochures and guides.

- *http://www.mcps.co.uk*
  Provides information about the Mechanical Copyright Protection Society which collects and distributes royalties on behalf of its members in the music industry and also negotiates agreements with those who wish to use musical works protected by copyright.

Appendix

- *http://www.prs.co.uk*
  Provides information about the Performing Rights Society which collects and distributes royalties on behalf of its members regarding the broadcast of musical works.

- *http://www.era.org.uk*
  Provides information about the Educational Recording Agency which operates a licensing scheme for the educational use of material protected by copyright. Includes frequently asked questions, information about costs and a downloadable information booklet.

Chapter 4

- *http://www.cipa.org.uk*
  The website for the Chartered Institute of Patent Agents which includes a database of patent agents in the UK and general advice.

- *http://www.itma.org.uk*
  The website for the Institute of Trade Mark Attorneys which includes a database of trade mark attorneys (searchable by region) and general advice and information.

Chapter 5

- *http://www.dca.gov.uk/civil/procrules_fin/*
  Information on the Civil Procedure Rules including the pre-action protocols.

Index

alternative dispute resolution (ADR), 111
anti-trust law, 80
application, 24
arbitral system, 81
assignment, 56

Centre for Effective Dispute Resolution, 81
Civil Procedure Rules (CPR), 101
   aims, 102–4
   pre-action protocols, 102, 105
collaboration agreements, 71–3
collection societies, 32
commercial licences, 74
Community trade mark applications, 24
Community unregistered design right (CUDR), 19, 21
confidentiality agreements, 46–7, 58–9
confidential information, 44
   importance of, 45
   protection of, 45–6
copyright, 28–9, 33
   assignments, 32–3
   infringement, 33–5
   protection, 31
Copyright, Designs and Patents Act 1988, 30, 50

database, 35
database right, 30, 36
Department of Trade and Industry (DTI), 71
design, definition of, 17
designs, 7, 142
   law, 16–17
dispute resolution, 100
domain names, 41–4, 86, 143
due diligence, 123

English law, 100
estoppel, 53
European Community Directive, 21

147

European Community Trade Mark (CTM) system, 21
European Patent Convention, 9
exclusive licence, 57

gene patents, 11
goodwill, 56

heads of agreement, 61–2

industrial property, 2
infringements, 15, 20, 27
 primary, 20
 secondary, 20
insurance, 113–14
intellectual property, 1, 2
 addresses, 41
 agreement, 55, 82
 contracts, 58, 80
 right infringement, 53
 rights, 2, 4–5, 9, 50, 55, 85, 88–9, 119
interim orders, 115–16
Internet Corporation for Assigned Names and Numbers (ICANN), 44

know-how, 44

Lambert Review, 70
legality, 79
letter of claim, 105
liability, 79

licence, 57
 exclusive, 57
 non-exclusive, 57
 sole, 57
licence of right, 21
licensee, 57
litigation, 81, 100

Madrid Protocol, 21–2
manufacturing agreements, 64–6
materials transfer agreements, 60
mediation, 104, 112

'new', 18
Nominet, 43
non-disclosure agreement (NDA), 92
non-exclusive licence – *see* licence, non-exclusive

Office for the Harmonisation of the Internal Market (OHIM), 17
options, 63

Part 36 offer, 103, 104
passing off, 28, 36–7
 elements of, 37–8
patent attorney, 87–8, 96
Patent Cooperation Treaty, 9
Patent Office (UK), 9, 12, 14, 15, 17, 22, 57

Index

Patent Office (European: EPO), 9, 12–13,
patents, 7, 9–10, 15, 56, 141
　infringement of, 16
Patents Act 1977, 53, 112
Patents Court, 108
primary infringements – *see* infringements, primary
principles of IP maintenance and management, 98
product, definition of, 17
prospective copyright, 33

registered:
　design, 19, 21
　rights, 7
　trade marks, 22, 142
research agreements, 66–7, 144
rights:
　database – *see* database rights
　exploitation, 73
　generated, 85
　intellectual property – *see* IP rights
　moral, 32
　owned, 85
　registered, 7, 58, 94
　semiconductor topography, 50
　unregistered, 7, 94
ring fence, 10, 16

secondary infringements – *see* infringements, secondary
seed material, 35
'semiconductor product', 50
Semiconductor Products (Protection of Topography) Regulations 1989, 50
semiconductor topography rights – *see* rights, semiconductor topography
sign, 27
sole licence – *see* licence, sole
stem cell patents, 12
supplementary protection certificate (SPC), 47–8

Trade Mark Act 1994, 21
trade marks, 22–3, 25, 27, 56
　infringement of, 27–8
　licensing, 25
　registration of, 24–5, 26
　types of, 22–3
trade mark attorney, 87–8, 96

unregistered rights, 7